# TASHIDING

# TASHIDING

## Beyond Earth and Sky

*The Gardens of Douglas & Tsognie Hamilton*

DOUGLAS HAMILTON JR.

PHOTOGRAPHY BY

NORMAN BARKER

ORO EDITIONS

Tashiding is one of the oldest and most
venerated monasteries in the historic Himalayan
Kingdom of Sikkim. Loosely translated,
the word means "a very auspicious place."
We appropriated the name for our auspicious place.

—DOUGLAS & TSOGNIE HAMILTON

# CONTENTS

# TASHIDING MAP

1 Teahouse & Lake
2 Conifer & Maple Garden
3 Main House
4 Courtyard Garden
5 Pool & Pool Pavilion
6 Aviary
7 Playhouse & Tube Slide
8 Peony Pavilion & Garden Mounds
9 Stone Bridge & Shrine
10 Japanese Gate & Gardens
11 Hillside Sanctuary & Woods
12 The Stone Steps

1

2

3

4

5

6

7

8

9

10

11

12

# FOREWORD

KATE MARKERT

*Executive Director, Hillwood Estate, Museum & Gardens*

OPPOSITE
*Climbing roses and hydrangeas in bloom on the arbors of the peony pavilion at Tashiding*

THIS VOLUME IS VERY DIFFERENT from many other garden books. Although it has beautiful photographs of a magnificent estate, it is unusual insofar as the narrative accompanying the images tells a multifaceted history far beyond a description of an idyllic site and its creation. There is no professional landscape architect representing the approach to the terrain. Instead, this is truly a love story, or perhaps many love stories: a storybook romance, a profound connection with the natural world, and deep bonds with places and families. All these strands are woven through this captivating narrative.

You know right from the start that this is not your typical American garden: it's called Tashiding. Named in honor of the most important monastery in the historic Himalayan Kingdom of Sikkim, Tashiding means "a very auspicious place." The reasons for its name and its unique blending of East and West, Asian sensibilities and Maryland countryside, are revealed through many sides of the story chronicled here. This book embraces this garden's complicated past and tells the tale of several generations of two families, stories of love and perseverance. In this recounting, there are many layers of history, international political intrigue, and romance,

all of which contribute to the richness of the result: a beautiful, one hundred–acre estate in northern Baltimore County that has a bucolic yet distinctly Eastern sensibility. It is a garden like no other.

Douglas and Tsognie Hamilton have been married for more than fifty years, twenty-five of them spent working together to create this unique house and garden. Their vision for Tashiding evolved over the decades and reflects their accumulated life experiences. The many facets of their commitment are evident: to this land, to their parents and ancestors, to their children and grandchildren, and to the trees, plants, mosses, ferns, rocks, water, turtles, fish, and birds found here. In this endeavor, they have remained true to themselves, allowing each of their very distinct spirits to imbue the place. Their happiness at Tashiding comes through in the calm that pervades every acre, as well as in the pride with which their achievement is brought to life in this volume.

Tashiding encompasses meadows; a stream with a beautiful stone bridge; a rocky ridge with a stone stair leading to the many trails above; manicured gardens of roses and peonies; a lake with a teahouse, colorful koi, turtles, and water plants; a beautiful swimming pool and pool house; an aviary; a children's playhouse and slide; and the handsome fieldstone house that melds a nineteenth-century section with the contemporary expansion. A place for strenuous hiking as well as quiet contemplation, Tashiding offers options for being in nature in many ways, at every time of year.

The serenity of this magnificent garden belies the years of intense work required to bring it to fruition: invasive shrubs and plants had to be cleared, the lake dredged, the house renovated and expanded (another story of passion and perseverance), a thousand trees planted, and tons of rock moved. It was a slow process of transformation, loving care, fine-tuning, and persistence that continues today, disclosed in Douglas Hamilton's personal account in these pages.

Accompanying this rich narrative are more than three hundred photographs by Norman Barker, professor of pathology and art as applied medicine at the Johns Hopkins University School of Medicine, and a photographer whose work is in the permanent collections of many distinguished museums. He became intrigued by Tashiding and photographed every part of the property in every season, in all its many moods. His portfolio of magnificent images became the impetus for this permanent record of the place.

The Hamiltons have created an exceptional garden and have shared it not only with their families, but, through this book, with all who are fascinated by distinctive landscapes and their makers. This thoughtful, thorough, and multidimensional account invites us to experience vicariously the fruits of their marvelous, lifelong collaboration.

OPPOSITE
*Roses in full bloom at Tashiding's peony pavilion*

# PREFACE

OPPOSITE
*Repurposed antique Japanese copper dragon fish, or* shachihoko, *flank the stone path leading from behind the house to the pool area. In Japan,* shachihoko *are usually found on the ridges of castles and other important buildings.*

FOLLOWING
*The far northern tip of the lake includes a stone watercourse with flowing spring water, a Japanese Kasuga lantern, moss-covered rocks set in a river rock beach, and a variety of plantings, including irises and a specimen Japanese maple.*

ALTHOUGH TSOGNIE AND I DESIGNED the gardens at Tashiding ourselves, the success of the garden owes much to collaboration with a wide variety of nurserymen and women, landscapers, arborists, stonemasons, horticulturalists, and others. Indeed, partnering with folks who make their living working with trees, plants, and stone has been a particular joy as we developed Tashiding's expansive and diverse gardens.

First among these helpful folks is Stanley "Hank" Beall, who joined us on a part-time basis shortly after we purchased Tashiding more than twenty-five years ago. Whatever the task—and there have been many as we set about creating the garden that exists today—Hank has met all challenges with enthusiasm, skill, and a can-do approach. He has worked hand in hand with me as we constructed berms, moved and placed rocks, cleared invasives, and set about transforming the property. He has an intuitive sense of design and has often collaborated with me on critical installations.

Nine years ago, Efrain Martinez Sosa joined us as our full-time gardener. Working both independently and in concert with Hank, who continues to work for us on a part-time basis,

Efrain is in large part responsible for the beautifully maintained presentation of the garden. His professionalism and attention to detail are unparalleled.

There are many stone elements in our garden, ranging from walls to bridges, steps, and other garden features. Two individuals and their teams are responsible for the great majority of this work. Andreas Grothe, a German immigrant and owner of New World Gardens, helped source and install much of the material we used in bridges, gardens, road surfaces, and pathways. Notably, he worked with us to move several 23,000-pound boulders (a gift from a generous neighbor) and install them in the conifer and maple garden. Andreas also collaborated with us to locate and install some of the first major plantings in the field that is now the west meadow.

Over the past two decades, Rob Stegman and his small crew at Stegman Stone Masonry have constructed all the stone walls at Tashiding. Rob and I located and purchased many dry-stacked stone walls from old farms located in the western part of Baltimore County. Loading and transporting hundreds of tons of this material was a laborious task involving lots of handwork (and perseverance). Notably, Rob and his team worked closely with me to install the stone steps that rise ten stories from the stream valley to the ridge above. The stone hardscape to which both Andreas and Rob have made such strong contributions forms the foundation of our gardens.

One of Tsognie's and my favorite activities as we developed our gardens involved touring local nurseries with Roland Harvey or his nephew Curry, of Natural Concerns, Inc. We set about these expeditions armed with multicolored tape (to mark the trees we selected), cell phones with cameras, and paper and pen. Most of the time, we selected trees because we liked their form, texture, or color. Rarely did we purchase a tree for a specific location. Only after we acquired our trees did we decide where to plant them. The survival of a transplanted tree owes much to the care taken in transporting, handling, and planting it after it has been purchased. We are indebted to Roland, Curry, and their excellent crews for their skill.

The late Bob Farmer of Gristmill Landscaping and Nursery shared his passion for Japanese maples with us and so many others in our circle of gardening friends. Bob became a cherished friend. We often think of him as we watch many of the varieties of maples he recommended grow and mature.

Maripat Neff and Mark Sullivan's Fieldstone Nursery has likewise been an excellent source for unusual conifers, maples, and other trees. Both Maripat and Mark hold graduate degrees in fine art from the Maryland Institute College of Art. Their artistic background is reflected in the variety and quality of trees and plants to be found in their nursery.

We are indebted to horticulturalist George Mozal of Clear Ridge Nursery; George inspects and helps identify and manage alien insects and plant diseases that are the bane of any gardener's existence. Many of our favorite installations include varieties of boxwood, which are subject to boxwood blight, a fungal disease prevalent in our area. Without George's care and attention, these and other areas of the garden would be very much in decline.

Contractor David Sutphen and his skilled team built not only the house but also most of the ancillary structures, including the aviary, peony pavilion, teahouse, and playhouse. The playhouse, located well up a hill, and the teahouse, with its underwater foundation and support, presented considerable logistical and technical challenges. David's enthusiastic team was always up to whatever challenge presented itself.

We also owe a debt of gratitude to the community of gardeners in our area who have shared their gardens with us and in so many ways encouraged our gardening pursuits. Early in our marriage, we often visited Breezewood, the country estate and gardens of the late Alexander B. Griswold, whose gardens in Monkton, Maryland, reflected his interest in Asian aesthetics. Jean Silber and her late husband, Sidney, whose superb Baltimore County gardens were a "must see" for any garden tour visiting central Maryland, blessed us with their friendship and many gifts of plant material, including a specimen China fir (*Cunninghamia lanceolata*), which has grown twenty-five feet in height and is now one of the outstanding trees in our garden.

Amy and Charles "Chuck" Newhall, creators of Brightside Gardens, have given us much moral support in recent years. Brightside Gardens pays homage to the Newhalls' extraordinary life journey and to themes of classical literature and philosophy. Penney and A. C. Hubbard's Walnut Hill is another exceptional and personal garden, which the Hubbards graciously open to garden groups and fellow gardeners. Visiting these gardens, all of which were well established years or decades before we began ours, has inspired us to create and expand our own very personal vision. Friend Jean Silber once observed that she never met a gardener who was not a nice person. And that has certainly been our experience.

# INTRODUCTION

The faith waiting in the heart of a seed
promises a miracle of life
which it cannot prove at once.

—RABINDRANATH TAGORE

THE GENESIS OF TASHIDING, our home and gardens in Maryland, began on a stifling and humid July morning in New Delhi, India, in 1972. I was several months shy of my twenty-second birthday. I had flown all night from Paris, arriving at the bustling Delhi airport at two in the morning, my first stop in what was to be four months of vagabonding through India and the Himalayan foothills, including a stay of many weeks in a Tibetan monastery. I had $800 in cash and traveler's checks, carried my sleeping bag and other possessions in my backpack, and had no credit cards. The era of cell phones was still decades in the future.

While in Paris planning my trip, I stayed with my Aunt Elaine Hamilton, an artist who had traveled extensively in South Asia. She provided me with a list of friends and acquaintances in India, Darjeeling, and Sikkim who she knew would be of help to me in my travels. My aunt was particularly close to the royal family of the mountainous Himalayan Kingdom of Sikkim.

Through my aunt's auspices, I already knew Princess Sodeun-la, a niece of the Sikkim Chogyal, or king. When I was in my early teens, Sodeun-la, five years my senior, spent several of her college summer breaks with my family in Maryland. She became like an older sister to me.

OPPOSITE
*Moss, rocks, and plantings in the courtyard garden, which is viewed from within the house. The design evokes the feeling of the Sikkim Himalayas.*

Although I had not seen her in years, her vivid descriptions of the Buddhist Himalayan world had excited my imagination and were in part responsible for my interest in traveling to the Indian subcontinent.

In the summer of 1972, Sodeun-la was working as an interior designer in New Delhi, putting the finishing touches on the newly constructed Sikkim House, which was to serve as the Sikkim Embassy. I was certain she would host me for a few days and help orient me to this new and, to me, exotic place.

It was still dark when I cleared customs and hired a cab to drive me through the heat and dust of the Indian night to the Sikkim House address in Delhi's Chanakyapuri neighborhood. I arrived at the gate just after sunrise. There, I was met by a security guard who, when I asked to see Princess Sodeun-la, informed me that she was in Hong Kong and was not expected back for at least a week. My heart sank as I realized I was now probably on my own. I pulled out my aunt's handwritten list of contacts, hoping for some measure of inspiration and good luck. My eyes settled on the name of a young Sikkimese woman who had stayed with my aunt in France earlier that summer and who was attending college in New Delhi. I knew little about her, other than that she had some connection to the palace in Sikkim.

I gave her name to the guard, who eyed me carefully, as if he wasn't certain whether to shoo me away. After an awkward pause, he nodded but told me she had not yet risen, certainly reasonable given the early hour. I gave him my name and he, allowing me to wait just inside the gate, agreed to have someone inform her of my presence when she awoke.

Thirty minutes later, a pretty young woman emerged from a small building located next to the unfinished main structure and walked toward me.

I was about to meet my destiny.

How to describe that first meeting with Tsognie Wangmo, the woman I was to marry, whom I have now known for more than fifty years? My first observation was her casual but stylish look. She wore fitted, bright-orange cotton slacks and a patterned chiffon top. Her python-skin platform shoes, which were then quite popular, made her look taller than her five-foot height. She hadn't had time to put on any makeup; sleep was still in her eyes. In the strong sun, tiny beads of perspiration formed on her nose. She introduced herself in fluent English, said they had expected me days earlier, then suggested we get out of the heat. She spoke in Hindi to the guards at the gate, and they quickly stepped aside.

OPPOSITE
*Tsognie, New Delhi, India, summer 1972*

ABOVE
*Tsognie and me at Emerald Hill, my family home in Maryland, October 1973, two weeks before our engagement*

Once inside, she spoke to a servant in Tibetan, ordering tea and toast. In less than two minutes, she had confidently taken command and spoken fluently in three languages—none of which were her native tongue—all while putting me completely at ease. Within hours I was completely besotted, and within days our bond of fifty years had been firmly established.

## The Nature of Sikkim

Tsognie's homeland, Sikkim, the middle and smallest of the three historical Himalayan Kingdoms, is nestled between Chinese Tibet to the north, India to the south, Bhutan to the east, and Nepal to the west. Located just twenty-seven degrees north of the equator, Sikkim ranges in elevation from 800 feet above sea level in the south to just over 28,000 feet above sea level at the peak of Kanchenjunga, the world's third-highest mountain. Sikkim's area is only a bit over 2,700 square miles, slightly larger than the state of Delaware. Despite its diminutive size, Sikkim's location and climate give rise to incredible biodiversity, among the richest in the world. In a one- or two-day trek, it is possible to pick an orange from a tree in the southern tropical zone and then eat it while navigating one's way across a glacier.

Sikkim is a naturalist's paradise. In the mid-nineteenth century, Joseph Hooker, a renowned British botanist, plant hunter, and explorer, spent several years in Sikkim, producing one of the most beautiful and important illustrated botanical books of the era, *The Rhododendrons of Sikkim-Himalaya*. During his several years in Sikkim, Hooker collected thousands of plant species, including dozens of rhododendrons, adding greatly to the appreciation and use of rhododendrons in British gardens. Hooker later became the director of Kew Gardens in London, a post he held from 1865 to 1885.

In 1898, botanists Sir George King and Robert Pantling published their seminal work, *The Orchids of the Sikkim-Himalaya*, illustrating 449 indigenous species of Sikkimese orchids. It is fair to say that anyone raised in the shadow of Kanchenjunga has a special relationship with Sikkim's distinct mountain environment.

What do these recollections have to do with a garden that we began twenty-five years after the events described earlier? Love fuels perseverance. After exchanging hundreds of letters and overcoming the hurdles of distance and cultural differences, Tsognie and I married in 1974. We honeymooned by trekking in the remote northern Sikkimese mountains to altitudes approaching 20,000 feet. Himalayan trekking involves multiple steep ascents followed by equally steep descents through forests of rhododendrons, firs, and pines. We traveled through temperate, alpine, and glacial zones, each with its own characteristics and distinct plant communities.

A love of the natural world became one of the foundations of our life as a couple. We prioritized cultural travel and exploration over material things. Tsognie did not learn

OPPOSITE
*Kanchenjunga mountain range, west central Sikkim*

RIGHT TOP
*Honeymoon trek, May 1974, Tsognie and me at the crest of Lungnak-la, just shy of 17,000 feet elevation*

RIGHT BOTTOM
*Tsognie navigates her way through a rhododendron forest in the rain, May 1972.*

FOLLOWING LEFT
*Title and sample pages of two notable mid-nineteenth-century botanical books:* The Rhododendrons of Sikkim-Himalaya *and* Illustrations of Himalayan Plants

FOLLOWING RIGHT
*Sikkimese prayer flags at Tashiding*

to drive or have a car until her early thirties when our two sons needed to be driven to school.

In the decades following our marriage, we undertook many treks in Sikkim, Nepal, and Bhutan. With our sons, Douglas III and Palden, we traveled extensively throughout Asia and Europe, exploring gardens in many different traditions. In creating Tashiding, we have given form to our interest in not only horticulture, but also art and the spiritual or religious world.

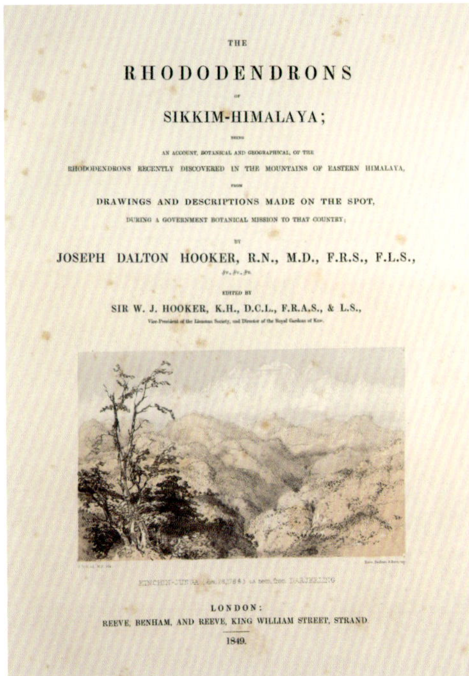
THE
RHODODENDRONS
OF
SIKKIM-HIMALAYA;
DRAWINGS AND DESCRIPTIONS MADE ON THE SPOT,
JOSEPH DALTON HOOKER, R.N., M.D., F.R.S., F.L.S.,
SIR W. J. HOOKER, K.H., D.C.L., F.R.A.S., & L.S.,
LONDON:
REEVE, BENHAM, AND REEVE, KING WILLIAM STREET, STRAND
1849.

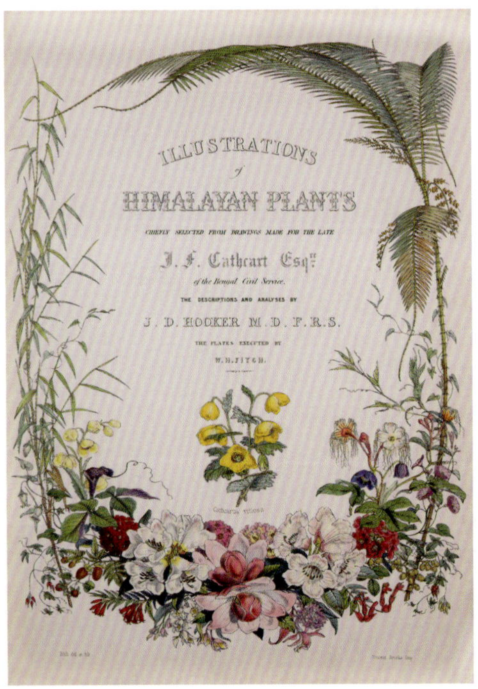
ILLUSTRATIONS
of
HIMALAYAN PLANTS
J. F. Cathcart Esq.
J. D. HOOKER M. D. F. R. S.

## Creating Tashiding

### *Eastern and Western Influences*

Tashiding reflects the cultural dichotomy of East and West, as well as the experiential and aesthetic journey we have pursued throughout our lives. The presence of prayer flags and other Eastern elements stirs curiosity. This is natural. Tsognie's Himalayan origin is interesting and, by most standards, exotic. Had I married a woman from Kenya or Italy or India, this would be a very different garden. Because we designed Tashiding's gardens ourselves, our creation is in a way a meditation or reflection on our lives and experiences, individually and as a couple.

Many people have visited Tashiding over the years. Most relate that when they drive up our driveway or walk through the garden they feel as though they have entered a refuge, a place with a pervasive spiritual presence. Some say their blood pressure drops. Although our gardens are indeed attractive, we rarely hear "This is really pretty." Visitors usually describe how they feel in the garden rather than how it looks.

The root of a garden, much like the root of a tree, may be hidden, but it provides the nourishment for all that can be seen. As self-described gardeners, we share an avocation enjoyed to varying degrees by millions of folks. Every person who creates a garden begins with a piece of land, a "vocabulary" of plant material available in their geographic and climatic region, and the great intangible—the seed of their own imagination. For us, who began with no plan and in fact never put pen to paper, it is easier, and quite revealing, to observe the fruits of our gardening efforts in retrospect. When asked how we made decisions relating to Tashiding, Tsognie and I often think about intuition informed by experience as a key element of the design process, the heart of our own seed.

# PART ONE

# THE ORIGIN STORY

CHAPTER ONE

# An American Family

PREVIOUS PAGE
*The house at Emerald Hill, circa 1960s, photographed in winter from across the farm pond*

OPPOSITE
*The renovated stone house at Emerald Hill, circa 1960s*

I WAS RAISED AT EMERALD HILL, our family's country property located in Maryland's Patapsco Valley, several miles west of Baltimore City. Emerald Hill was a derelict thirty-five-acre property when my paternal grandparents and their three young adult children pooled their resources to acquire it in 1940. At the time of acquisition, the existing dilapidated stone house lacked plumbing and other amenities. Over the next several decades, the family, with their own hands, updated the house, constructed bathrooms, built garages and stables, added a lake, and constructed a swimming pool. My extended family—my paternal grandparents; my parents, Douglas Sr. and Margaret; Aunt Sparky and Uncle Bruce and their children, Lydia, Bruce, and Lee; plus my sister Wendy and I—lived in the old house until 1955, when my father built a house on the property for his young family. In 1959, my sister Nell (Helen Margaret) was born. As I neared my tenth birthday, in 1960, Emerald Hill had the look of a rather grand country estate.

In many respects, Emerald Hill was a protective cocoon in which my siblings, my cousins, and I were nurtured by parents, grandparents, aunts, and uncles. At the same time, it was a window to a larger and more diverse world. My mother, Margaret, was born in Scotland in 1929 and immigrated to the United States in 1949 to seek new opportunities. She was a child of both

the British Empire and of the privations of World War II. She once described the joy she felt upon eating her first orange, a rare treat in Scotland during the war years. My childhood was filled with colorful Kipling stories set in India, a deep reverence for Winston Churchill, and accounts of Lord Carnarvon and Howard Carter's discovery of Tutankhamun's tomb. My mother's summer gardens were filled with flowers, as was her greenhouse in winter.

My father, Douglas Sr., was industrious, practical, and hardworking. He and his siblings came of age during the Great Depression, when money and opportunity were in short supply. But he had the Hamilton trait of making something out of nothing. In 1939, at the age of twenty-one, he won the Eastern United States figure skating championship in Madison Square Garden in New York. Against his parents' wishes and without their knowledge, he earned a pilot's license while still a teen. He once buzzed his parents' house, returning home to his father's comments about "some damned fool" almost crashing an airplane into the house. Later, when he admitted he was the pilot and after the predicted admonishments, his mother asked him to take her for her inaugural flight. The first thing she wanted to do when in the air was to buzz her sister's house.

My father chased foxes with the Howard County Hunt Club and registered a patent for an airplane propeller while working for Koppers Company, a major Baltimore manufacturer he had joined in 1935, right out of high school. All this he did by the age of thirty.

## The World of My Youth

My extended family at Emerald Hill took great pride in their self-sufficiency. Until my father and uncle decided it was too much work, we raised pigs, steer, and chickens for our own consumption. We also had a cow for milk, butter, and cheese. A large vegetable garden provided food in season, and large quantities of vegetables were frozen and canned to sustain the family in winter. As a boy, I plucked chickens, salted hams, and shelled lima beans by the bushel.

My Grandma Hamilton, when in her upper sixties, built with her own hands a stone cottage in the woods several hundred yards from the two main houses. She did all the stonework, assisted only by a single farmhand who helped her gather fieldstones and mix cement. She eventually moved in, announcing that throughout her marriage, which began in 1915, her husband liked to sleep with the windows closed and in her final years she wanted to sleep with them open. Most evenings, my grandfather walked up from the old house to join her for dinner.

A regular treat enjoyed by us children was to join Grandma for a breakfast of bacon, eggs, and buttered toast cooked in a cast-iron skillet on a wood fire just outside her cottage. All but the toast was produced at Emerald Hill. When Grandma died in 1980, my grandparents had been married for sixty-five years and had never lived apart from their two sons, Douglas and Bruce. The Hamilton family found strength in working together.

OPPOSITE

*My parents, Douglas Sr. and Margaret Hamilton, with the family woodie at Emerald Hill, winter 1950*

RIGHT

*Hamilton mothers and children, pictured on the lawn of the original house at Emerald Hill in the early 1950s. From left, my aunt, Lydia "Sparky" Hamilton, holding her youngest daughter, Lee, with son, Bruce (my lifelong business partner), and older daughter, Lydia, to his right. On the right, my mother, Margaret, holds my sister Wendy, with me seated to her left. We all lived together until my parents' house on the property was completed in 1955.*

# THE HAMILTONS *of* EMERALD HILL

THE HAMILTONS, my paternal ancestors, immigrated to Baltimore from Strathaven in Lanarkshire, Scotland, shortly after the turn of the nineteenth century. Unlike many immigrants, the Hamiltons seem to have been moderately affluent. They set up a furniture manufacturing business in the Fells Point neighborhood in Baltimore. Shortly after, they purchased a large farm in Mount Washington, a village located along the Jones Falls, just north of the city, where they farmed and established a lumber mill, importing hardwoods from Central America. Family records indicate that they continued to sell rental properties in Scotland into the 1860s.

Beginning in the 1890s, my great-grandfather James Hamilton (1859–1938) began to display traits that would manifest themselves in future generations. In search of adventure and gold, he joined in the Klondike Gold Rush of 1896–99, returning to Baltimore after a lengthy absence with stories of adventure and Native American artifacts but little gold. He then began to construct greenhouses to further his interest in horticulture. His hobby eventually became a successful business. From the early 1900s through 1960, the Hamilton Nurseries were the largest wholesale nursery in the city.

James Hamilton had seven children—five boys and two girls. My grandfather Robert Bruce Hamilton Sr., born in 1887, inherited his father's charm but less of his entrepreneurial talent. His marriage in 1915 to my grandmother, Lee Elmer Wood, proved fortuitous. Grandma Hamilton was a force of nature, possessing the gift of making something out of nothing. Their children—my Uncle Bruce, Douglas Sr. (my father), and my Aunt Elaine—were born in 1916, 1918, and 1920, respectively. Money was often in short supply, but Grandma's industriousness and imagination served the family well during difficult times.

About 1924, the family rented Blackshears, a farm of several hundred acres just west of Baltimore. This was the family home for the next sixteen years, including during the Great Depression. To survive during this period, the family boarded horses and took lodgers into their home.

Each summer for most of the 1920s, they rented out the house at Blackshears to Baltimore residents who wished to escape the heat of the city. The family relocated to a campground they called Camp Copperhead, in what is now known as the Patapsco Valley State Park. They had a large kitchen tent, a living room tent with a piano, and sleeping tents. A nearby stream was dammed to create a swimming hole, complete with an improvised showerhead. Camp life captured the values my grandmother inculcated in her three children: self-sufficiency, resourcefulness, resilience, and cooperation. These are the values that shaped the Hamiltons through the twentieth century and beyond.

OPPOSITE

*My grandfather, an amateur photographer, chronicled camp life with a series of glass negatives, which are still in my possession. In my favorite of these photographs, which dates to about 1925, Grandma sits on a rustic bridge spanning the stream just above the swimming hole. My Uncle Bruce sits to the left of my father, who is in the middle, with Aunt Elaine on the right. The board dam they built is clearly seen in the foreground.*

# The World Widens

My father's sister, Elaine, sought her destiny away from home, but Emerald Hill and the family remained her touchstone throughout her life. Beginning in 1946, her development as a serious painter well underway, she split her time between the Art Students League in New York and the Instituto Allende in San Miguel de Allende, Mexico. In 1953, she relocated to Italy, where she lived and worked primarily in Florence and Milan. From 1960 onward she lived either in Paris or its environs, with extended stays in Pakistan, Japan, India, Nepal, and Sikkim. She didn't want children herself but saw it as her responsibility to share her world with her nieces and nephews.

Throughout her life, Elaine often appeared at Emerald Hill with international guests in tow. In 1958, she arrived with her close friend, Guglielmo Raggiotti, who as a teen during World War II had fought with the Italian resistance. Guglielmo was accompanied by his friend Mario Sereni, a baritone who had recently debuted with the Metropolitan Opera in New York. When he sang for the family in the library of the old house, the glasses in the cabinets shook. From that moment, the course of my seven-year-old cousin Lee's life was set. She went on to a successful career as a soprano in the esteemed Metropolitan Opera chorus.

In the summer of 1962, at Elaine's initiation, the crown prince of Sikkim, Palden Thondup Namgyal, arrived for a week's stay with his American fiancée, Hope Cooke. Who could have predicted that his oldest daughter, who at age ten was attending boarding school in Kalimpong in the Himalayan foothills, would years later set the course for so much of my own life?

Over the next several summers, the crown prince's niece, Princess Sodeun-la, spent her college summer breaks at Emerald Hill. I became her very curious little brother.

In the summer of 1966, when I was fifteen and my two oldest cousins, Bruce and Lydia, were sixteen and seventeen, our parents funded a ten-week journey with Elaine to trace Mediterranean and European history, art, and culture. Our sojourn began in Egypt, continued through Jordan and the Holy Land by horse, camel, and Land Rover, then was followed by introductions to the civilizations and wonders of Turkey, Greece, Italy, Austria, France, and Britain. I turned sixteen in October of that year.

That Christmas, to my parents' consternation, Aunt Elaine presented me with an illustrated copy of Vatsyayana's *Kama Sutra*. It deepened my interest in the Indian subcontinent and introduced me to the ethical and emotional aspects of Eastern erotic love.

The next spring, I began my working life as a member of the outdoor maintenance crew of a business park. With $1,000 borrowed from my father—it took three summers of work to pay him back—I purchased a used 1962 MGA sports car, red with red leather seats. Emerald Hill had set a firm foundation for all that was to follow, and the world seemed ripe for the taking.

OPPOSITE,
CLOCKWISE FROM LEFT
*Summer 1966: My cousin Lydia and I tease our Palestinian guide in Wadi Rum in the Jordanian desert; houses carved in hoodoo rock formations in Cappadocia, central Turkey; Colossi of Memnon, near Luxor, Egypt*

RIGHT
*Souvenir postcards*

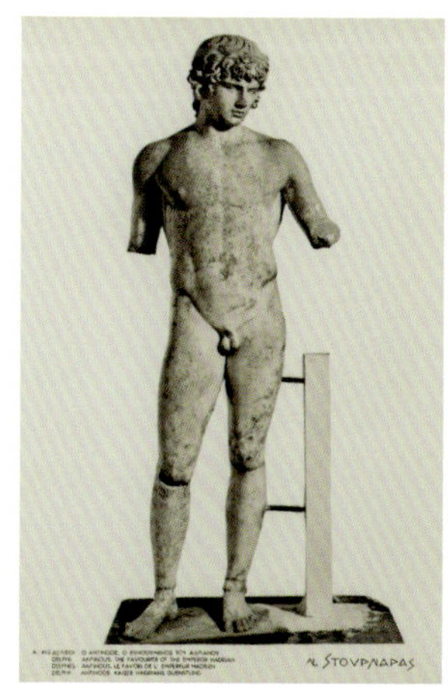

# ELAINE HAMILTON (1920–2010)

ASIDE FROM MY PARENTS, no adult had more influence on the trajectory of my life than my father's younger sister, Elaine Hamilton, an accomplished artist and citizen of the world. Although American born and raised, she spent her life far removed from the land of her birth. Her artistic vision was informed by the places she lived, the incredibly diverse friendships she developed throughout the world, and the myriad experiences that resulted from a willingness to place herself in challenging new environments.

She lived most of her life in a man's world, a world in which she traveled comfortably, creating for herself significant opportunities and associations even in places where women's roles had been historically limited, such as Mexico, Pakistan, and Japan.

Beginning in the late 1940s, she split her time between the Art Students League in New York and the National Polytechnic Institute in Mexico City, where she also worked as an apprentice to noted muralist David Alfaro Siqueiros. Later she moved to San Miguel de Allende, where she immersed herself in Mexican life and built a house as she continued to study and paint. Her Mexican paintings were featured in one-artist shows at the Baltimore Museum of Art in 1951 and the Galería de Arte Moderno in Mexico City in 1952.

Elaine won a Fulbright scholarship to Italy in 1952, and lived in Italy for seven years, developing close friendships with architect Gio Ponti and his family, sculptor

Arnaldo Pomodoro, and famed travel writer and ethnologist Fosco Maraini. While in Italy, her artistic style moved decisively to abstract expressionism, or action painting, which the French refer to as Tachisme. Among the galleries that featured her work during this period were the Galleria del Milione in Milan and the Galleria San Marco in Rome. In 1956 and 1958, her works were included in the Italian pavilion at the Venice Biennale.

In 1960, Elaine moved to France, her base for the next forty years. At the same time, her attention was increasingly oriented eastward, to Pakistan, India, the Himalayas, and Japan. In late 1959 and early 1960, she spent three months painting in Pakistan, followed by a major exhibition in Karachi, sponsored by the Arts Council of Pakistan.

In the same year, at age forty, Elaine organized a trek deep into the Karakoram range of the western Himalayas. It would be the first of many such Himalayan expeditions over the next fifteen years, both in Pakistan and Nepal. She traveled alone, often for a month or more, accompanied only by a retinue of native porters.

She traveled frequently in India and the Himalayas during this period, eventually meeting and befriending members of Sikkim's royal family. Elaine was particularly close to the crown prince of Sikkim, Palden Thondup Namgyal, who would years later play a major role in my life as my father-in-law.

OPPOSITE

*Elaine Hamilton on the Khumbu Glacier, near Mount Everest, 1967.*

RIGHT

*An early and important commission, 1950. Elaine works on a large mural at the Instituto Allende depicting scenes and prominent figures from Mexican history.*

Back in France, she met Michel Tapié, the French art critic, exhibition organizer, and collector. Tapié was a champion of Elaine's work, organizing numerous exhibitions of her art in France, Italy, and Japan. In Japan, she was hosted by artist Sofu Teshigahara and became one of only two Western artists invited to exhibit with the Gutai group, an avant-garde art movement considered one of the most important in the decades following the end of World War II. In April 1961, she had a solo exhibition at the Fujikawa Gallery in Osaka.

Exhibitions at many galleries in Europe continued through the 1960s and '70s, including the Galerie Stadler in Paris and the Galleria d'Arte Cortino in Milan, where her work was shown alongside that of Hans Hofmann, Franz Kline, and Lee Krasner, as well as many of the other leading abstract painters of her generation. Her circle of artist friends in France included Man Ray and Paul Jenkins.

Although New York was the center of abstract painting throughout the 1960s, Elaine had little appetite for the vagaries and politics of the New York art market, which explains why her extraordinary work is better known in other places in the world. Her painting was both individualistic and uncompromising. She wrote, "I often return to the 'abode of the snows' for it seems there my thoughts crystallize into forms that find their way into the movements and rhythm pulsating in and out of my canvases."

OPPOSITE
*Tsognie and I view the San Miguel mural in October 2023. This painting is considered an important work in the art history of the Mexican state of Guanajuato.*

LEFT
*Elaine is credited with introducing abstract expressionism to Pakistan. While there in early 1960, she completed a large body of work, including this piece, which was included in a major exhibition of her paintings in Karachi, sponsored by the Arts Council of Pakistan.*

ABOVE
*One of the paintings Elaine completed in Japan in 1961 as a member of the Gutai group. This work was included in a one-person show at the Fujikawa Gallery in Osaka that year.*

LEFT

*One of a pair of paintings rendered in black and white, which won the Menton Prize in France in 1968.*

My work is depth, projection, and pulsation. These works are created through me. There is a communion of infinite energy, particles, writings, and cataclysmic forms—sound energy, sense energy, and most importantly, spiritual energy.

—ELAINE HAMILTON

CHAPTER TWO

# Tashiding's Sikkimese Influence

Travel is fatal to prejudice . . .

—MARK TWAIN

OPPOSITE
*Stone pathway and bridge crossing the stream at Tashiding.*

ON JANUARY 26, 1950, the new constitution of independent India went into effect, and the day was then and thereafter celebrated as Republic Day. India marked the first Republic Day with parades, school holidays, and numerous cultural performances by groups from all over India, including the Indian protectorate of Sikkim.

An eighteen-year-old Sikkimese woman, Kaden Shipmo, a member of Sikkim's indigenous Lepcha people, traveled to New Delhi with a song and dance team for the celebration. Kaden was the second oldest of nine children born to Chungu Shipputso and his wife, Pemkit. (Female members of the family are known as Shipmo and male members as Shipputso.) Kaden and many of her siblings would go on to play important leadership roles in Sikkim's modern history. Kaden's brother, recounting Shipputso family lore, relates that family members are descendants of the "third of the seven superhuman or wandering spirits from the East named Phim-Choo-Raam."

Most important to this narrative is that Kaden was the lover of Sikkim's dashing twenty-six-year-old crown prince, Palden Thondup Namgyal.

The same month Kaden performed in New Delhi, and half a world away, my twenty-year-old Scottish mother, Margaret, and my father, Douglas, thirty-one, married and settled into life at Emerald Hill. I was born in late October of that year.

By the time of my birth, Kaden was expecting the prince's first child. Tsognie was born in Gangtok, Sikkim, in May 1951. She quickly became the apple of everyone's eye. Sikkimese place great importance on a person's horoscope, which is calculated by monks upon the birth of a baby. Tsognie was born in the Year of the Iron Rabbit, according to the Tibetan lunar calendar. Her horoscope stated: she will be a harmonious person who will love her sons and she will be attracted to flowers and pleasant fragrances; she will be skillful, intelligent, hardworking, and will love performing charity; and she may not stay at her birthplace all her life. It also said that the most important acts she must perform in life are to receive empowerment from high lamas (monks) and be compassionate to all living creatures. (I did not see Tsognie's horoscope until years after our marriage. Its accuracy in predicting both her character and her life's journey seemed remarkable to me.)

## Tsognie's Early Years

Though devout Buddhists, Tsognie's parents decided that her interests would be best served by enrolling her in St. Joseph's Convent School, an English-language school in Kalimpong, a hill station located across the border in India, about a three-hour drive across mountain roads from Sikkim's capital of Gangtok. At age six, Tsognie entered St. Joseph's as a boarding student. She spoke not a word of English. "How did you manage?" I asked her years later. "I learned quickly," she laughed. Her teachers were mainly Catholic nuns from Western countries. It was the first of Tsognie's many adaptations in life.

Close to the mountain passes that led through Sikkim and the Tibetan frontier, Kalimpong was an important outpost for trade between India and Tibet. Caravans of colorful pack animals carrying wool, grains, and furs to and from Tibet were much in evidence during Tsognie's time at St Joseph's. By the late 1950s, large numbers of Tibetan refugees escaping China's occupation arrived in Kalimpong. In 1962, China closed the border with Tibet and trade ended. By then, at the insistence of Tsognie's father, she had transferred to Mount Hermon School in Darjeeling, one of the best-known hill stations, founded a century earlier by the British. He wanted her to have coeducational schooling, and Mount Hermon was a Methodist coeducational boarding school.

This transfer suited Tsognie very well. A self-described tomboy, she preferred the company of boys to the intrigues that preoccupied many of her female classmates. At Mount Hermon, she distinguished herself academically and as an athlete. An outstanding field hockey player, she was also the girls' 100- and 200-meter sprinting champion of her school. And, at barely five feet tall, she was also the girls' shot-put champion.

From Mount Hermon, Tsognie could look north to Sikkim and the snow-covered Kanchenjunga massif, thirty miles away as the crow flies. Tsognie was one of a handful of students to take the rigorous climbing course at Darjeeling's renowned Himalayan Mountaineering Institute. There, under the guidance of Sherpas Tenzing Norgay, who along with Edmund Hillary was the first to climb Mount Everest, and Nawang Gombu, the first man to climb Everest twice, Tsognie mastered rock climbing and rappelling skills. My years of exploring Emerald Hill's forests, pastures, and stream valleys seemed tame by comparison.

## Into the Himalayas

Soon after Tsognie and I first met in New Delhi in 1972, I spent a couple of weeks in Darjeeling, about a dozen miles north of Sonada, location of the Tibetan monastery where I studied. With a single guide, I trekked from Darjeeling through tea gardens and remote villages for several days to Sandakphu, the highest point on the Singalila range at close to 13,000 feet elevation and the highest point in West Bengal. Sandakphu offered an extraordinary view of Kanchenjunga. After spending the night in a small bungalow

OPPOSITE, LEFT TO RIGHT
*Circa 1950: Kaden Shipmo sitting raised at the left elbow of India's first president, Rajendra Prasad (center, seated); Crown Prince Palden Thondup Namgyal; Kaden Shipmo.*

ABOVE
*A southern Sikkim village surrounded by rice paddies. Tibetans refer to Sikkim as* Denjong, *which means "valley of rice."*

near the peak of Sandakphu, I woke at four in the morning to watch the sun rise over Kanchenjunga, my first view of the mountain, which until that point had been shrouded in monsoon clouds. At first, all I could see of the mountain was a massive, dark silhouette. As the sun came up, the eastern faces of the mountain turned bright orange, almost the color of flame. Hours passed, the sun climbed higher, and the mountain turned from orange to bright white against the azure sky. This scene evoked in me an overwhelming emotional reaction. I had gained a deeper understanding of Tsognie's worldview, a vision of the natural world that we increasingly saw through the same eyes.

By the autumn of 1972, after months of traveling throughout India and Sikkim, I had run out of money. Before departing for home, though, I had the opportunity to visit Tsognie in Delhi for another ten days. Our parting was filled with sorrow. The prospects for us meeting again seemed remote.

I flew to France to spend two weeks with my Aunt Elaine before returning home to Maryland to begin a career. What I really wanted was to return to Asia and Tsognie as fast as possible.

After I'd been home a month, my father asked if I might be interested in joining the family business on a trial basis. The family firm, founded in 1950 by my father and my Uncle Bruce, provided contract machining and assembly services to an array of firms. Unfortunately, an attempt to develop new proprietary products in the late 1960s had not succeeded, saddling the firm with debt that threatened its viability. Operating losses were being funded by loans from my father and uncle's personal savings. My cousin Bruce, my uncle's son, joined the firm soon after I did. Shortly after, his father, a brilliant designer and machinist, underwent successful heart bypass surgery and retired.

Coming in as an outsider, even with no business experience, allowed me to see the company's weaknesses from a fresh perspective. For a year, I studied every aspect of the business. In the spirit of "necessity is the mother of invention" and with Bruce's strong support, I developed a comprehensive plan to restore the company to profitability and to retire the debt. In what I later recognized as a leap of faith, my father, though skeptical, gave me the go-ahead. Within eighteen months we eliminated the debt and returned the company to profitability.

At age twenty-four, I began running the company. I learned to trust my intuition. Bruce and I went on to acquire several other companies over the next fifteen years. Eventually, we closed the machining and contract manufacturing business and

ABOVE
*Young monks with me at Samdrub Darjay Chöling Monastery, Sonada (11 miles south of Darjeeling in the Himalayan foothills), September 1972.*

OPPOSITE
*Tsognie and me in Japan, 2014*

transformed the company into a profitable middle-market manufacturer, producing proprietary filter and respirator test equipment, elevator suspension systems, and pressure washers. Fulfilling the aspirations of our fathers, Bruce and I built a thriving business, a success our fathers lived to see.

Thirty-eight years later, in 2012, my focus was increasingly on developing the gardens at Tashiding and doing nonprofit work, including a term as board president of Baltimore's esteemed Walters Art Museum. My eldest son, Douglas III, had joined the firm about a decade earlier, successfully managing the elevator business. Aware of my many distractions, he came into my office one day and said, "Dad, I'm ready." He was thirty-five. I said, "Douglas, yes you are." I retired immediately, and, with Bruce's consent, appointed Douglas as CEO the next day. As was true when I joined the firm, authority is taken, not given. Douglas has gone on to reinvent and grow the companies in ways I could not have.

Bruce and I, partners for almost forty years, never had a serious disagreement. Our relationship was deeply rooted in the soil and goodwill of our upbringing together at Emerald Hill. Our family tended to march to the beat of its own drum, and Bruce and I were no exception. We never squandered our energy on conflict or drama.

## Marriage and Family

Not surprisingly, I married a woman who likewise marched to her own unique drum. Tsognie and I married in the spring of 1974. She had the option to work if she chose, but quickly realized that no employer would allow her five or more weeks per year to travel home to Sikkim. This, in fact, suited me quite well. Early in our marriage, I often traveled on sales trips up and down the East Coast, and Tsognie usually joined me. It enabled her to see something of her adopted country, and I felt as though we were on an extended honeymoon.

Back in Baltimore, Tsognie was quick to establish ground rules for the life she wanted. She joined me several times at business dinners with suppliers and customers. These could be tedious, but I believed they were necessary to develop the business. After one such evening, we arrived home and Tsognie announced that she would never attend another. This was not how she wanted to live her life. Upset at first, I explained to her that this was how business was conducted in America. She said if that was so then she would do without. The reality was that I did not particularly enjoy these evenings either. Reluctantly, I reduced and ultimately stopped such after-hours entertainment. I found it didn't make any difference to the success of my business.

Our world and family expanded considerably when Tsognie gave birth to our sons, Douglas III in 1977 and Palden in 1980. Douglas was the first grandchild on either side of our families. From the time they were infants, our sons traveled with us, first to India and Sikkim and later on extended trips throughout Asia and Europe.

We wanted our boys to experience many different cultures, peoples, and histories. My job enabled me to travel for extended periods. And traveling as a family allowed each of us to expand and deepen our worldview together. By the time Douglas and Palden went off to college, they had been around the world more than ten times. No single place, individual, or experience makes us who we are. When we accomplish or create something worthwhile, we can often find our inspiration in personal history, culture, family, and friends. It has certainly been so for Tsognie and me as we continue to refine all that is Tashiding.

# TREKKING *the* HIMALAYAS

TSOGNIE AND I CELEBRATED our marriage in 1974 by trekking in the isolated mountains of northwestern Sikkim. Twelve years passed before we had the opportunity to venture into the mountains again. Our second trip was as special as the first. In 1986, our sons, Douglas III and Palden, ages eight and five, joined us for a rigorous four-day trek in Bhutan, traveling from Bhutan's capital of Thimphu across the mountains to the town of Paro. Both sons proved their mettle by trekking through rain and sleet on one particularly difficult day. From Paro, we climbed up to Paro Taktsang, often referred to as Tiger's Nest, a small monastery that clings to a vertical rock face.

Tiger's Nest acquired both its name and sanctity from the ninth-century journey of Indian *vajra* master Padmasambhava, who introduced Buddhism to Tibet and the Himalayan kingdoms of Sikkim and Bhutan. He is believed to have flown from place to place on the back of a tiger: the locations where he landed are revered today as important pilgrimage sites. Many of these are found in remote valleys and mountain locations accessible only by rigorous treks, often of many days.

Our next two treks were far longer, higher, and more arduous than our Bhutan experience. In 1994, as a family, we trekked from the town of Yuksom in western Sikkim to Yangdzothang, a round trip of almost two weeks. Yuksom is the site where the first Sikkim Chogyal (king) was consecrated in 1642. Yangdzothang, at about 16,000 feet

elevation, affords a spectacular view of Kanchenjunga and the surrounding mountains, which flank the valley on all sides. A cave near the isolated valley of Yangdzothang is another Padmasambhava pilgrimage site.

A Himalayan expedition of this duration requires a significant amount of logistical planning. We traveled with twelve porters, a cook, and a cook's assistant. While traveling by jeep from Sikkim's capital of Gangtok to Yuksom, our cook purchased half a dozen chickens, which he intended to slaughter and cook several days into the trek. After arriving at our starting point, Tsognie, out of compassion, let all the chickens go. I suspect the villagers in Yuksom ate well the next night!

In 1999, at the urging of Douglas III, now age twenty-two, and Palden, nineteen, we repeated the challenging Yangdzothang trek. There could be no better beginning to their lives as independent young men. We know the richness of the Sikkimese mountains and alpine forests are forever etched in their memories. Our many Sikkim experiences remain at the forefront of our thoughts as Tsognie and I continue to shape our gardens at Tashiding.

OPPOSITE
*Our camp on the slope leading up to Thay-la, 1974.*

RIGHT
*Twenty years later, our camp at Yangdzothang, near the base of Kanchenjunga, 1994.*

TOP

*Our porters constructing a pole and bark lean-to, 1974.*

BOTTOM LEFT

*Palden, Douglas III, and me at Yangdzothang.*

BOTTOM RIGHT

*Palden, Tsognie, and Douglas III by a glacial lake at Yangdzothang, 1999.*

OPPOSITE

*A bamboo bridge provides the only way across a river in western Sikkim.*

CHAPTER THREE

# The House & Its Surroundings

OPPOSITE
*Tashiding, looking north from the lake to the house; on the right, the playhouse rises in the forest above the house, with the peony pavilion near the lake in the foreground.*

THE HOUSE AT TASHIDING has its origins in a house Tsognie and I built decades earlier. In 1979, wanting our two young sons to be raised in a rural environment, we purchased a tract of land in the community of Monkton, in northeastern Baltimore County. In 1983, we completed a lovely small house heavily influenced by Japanese aesthetics and architecture. It was located on a forested site on the southern slope of a hill overlooking the Gunpowder River valley. In that house, we raised our sons to adulthood and independence.

At a time when most empty nesters begin to contemplate scaling down, we (I, in particular) anticipated how the next chapter of our lives would evolve. The Monkton house was small and afforded limited space to display our growing art collections. Accessibility was a major concern. The garage was located seventy-five yards up the hill from the house. The road and path leading down to the house were steep and almost impossible to navigate in snowy or icy conditions. There were no water features on the property nor space to allow for gardening on the scale I envisioned. Accommodating older guests was increasingly difficult, and Tsognie and I, though still full of energy, were not getting any younger ourselves.

# OUR FIRST HOUSE (1983)

WHEN TSOGNIE AND I BUILT our Japanese-inspired house, which she calls Bay Yul, or "hidden land," we had never been to Japan. Our travels from the early 1970s through the early '80s were focused almost entirely on Sikkim.

Early in our marriage, dear friends lent us a copy of *Japanese Traditional Gardens* by Yoshinobu Yoshinaga. The gardens illustrated in this volume were new and exotic on one hand yet familiar on the other. Tsognie and I immediately commenced building our collection of books on Japanese aesthetics, architecture, and art. To us, the Japanese seemed to have distilled much of what we valued in the natural world into important aspects of their cultural identity. Our collections of Japanese lacquer, painting, ceramics, and metalwork are an outgrowth of this early exposure.

LEFT
*Looking up toward the courtyard of Bay Yul from below the house.*

OPPOSITE
*The southern elevation of Bay Yul after a winter snow.*

FOLLOWING LEFT
*Architect Jim Grieves's hand-drawn elevations for the reimagined house at Tashiding.*

FOLLOWING RIGHT
*A twilight three-quarter view of the Tashiding house's north elevation, showing a partial view of the stone steps leading down to the pool, which is just out of sight to the left.*

Tsognie and I knew we wanted to incorporate aspects of traditional Japanese architecture into the house we planned to build on the forested site in Monkton. We placed a query in *Fine Homebuilding* magazine and were contacted by architect Barbara Sandrisser and her partner, Peter Paul, of the Paul Partnership in New York City. Their enthusiasm for our project was as great as our own. The house that resulted from our collaboration, constructed on a very tight budget, included covered verandas and hand-planed custom doors, windows, and sliding shoji screens. The exterior Port Orford cedar fasciae, soffits, and trim boards were left to weather naturally. The roof was of traditional Japanese ceramic tile.

The most important aspect of the house for Tsognie, however, was neither its architecture nor the materials used in its creation, but rather that Dodrupchen Rinpoche, one of the preeminent masters of the Nyingma tradition of Tibetan Buddhism, had sanctified the site before we broke ground. The rituals he performed were to rebalance the forces of nature we would disturb by constructing the house. We continue to own and maintain Bay Yul as a guesthouse for friends when they visit Maryland.

By the time we began to develop the gardens at Tashiding decades later, we had visited Japan numerous times, taking special care to visit many of the extraordinary gardens we had come to admire through our extensive library of books on Japanese gardening.

# The Tashiding Vision

In 1998, a property in the Western Run Valley, about ten miles southwest of our Monkton house, came on the market. What the property had that appealed was a beautifully sited farmhouse built of hand-hewn limestone quarried on the site, a centrally located lake, a wonderful but trash-filled stream, and a nice mix of meadow, open fields, and forest. The bones were good but, sadly, the overall appearance was rather dismal.

The house oozed with charm and decay in equal measure—it had been neglected, to say the least. The broken-down farmhouse was largely uninhabitable. The main part of the house had been constructed beginning about 1818 by Quaker Jesse Scott, whose father and extended family joined other Quaker families in settling the Western Run Valley starting in the late eighteenth century. An 1842 addition, which followed the line of the original house, was built on fill and on grade (meaning it had no underground foundation), with the result that one corner of the house had settled almost a foot into the ground. The stone wall under the window closest to this sunken corner had ruptured and was bowing out eight or nine inches. The floor in the first-level room of the addition was eleven inches lower at one end, across a twenty-foot diagonal, than the other corner. The original windows, many of which had been painted shut for years, were rotten and insect infested. An added feature of the house was the presence of two large black snakes, whose shed skins were in ample display both in the root cellar under the house and in the attic.

Friends of ours had some years earlier successfully reimagined and enlarged a stone farmhouse located at the other end of the valley. Within a day of viewing the property, I contacted them for advice. They kindly referred me to Baltimore-based architect James R. "Jim" Grieves, who had worked with them on their project. At my request, Jim joined me the next day in surveying the existing house. While touring the dark and dank farmhouse, I described in broad terms the house I envisioned, one filled with light and air but respecting as much as possible the existing historical structure as part of a considerably larger and more modern house. I learned through our conversation that Jim had designed the exquisite Brandywine Museum in Chadds Ford, Pennsylvania. Tsognie and I had frequently visited and admired the museum's architecture and aesthetic sensibility. Jim's design for the Brandywine involved incorporating an old stone barn into a state-of-the-art museum of regional American art and illustration.

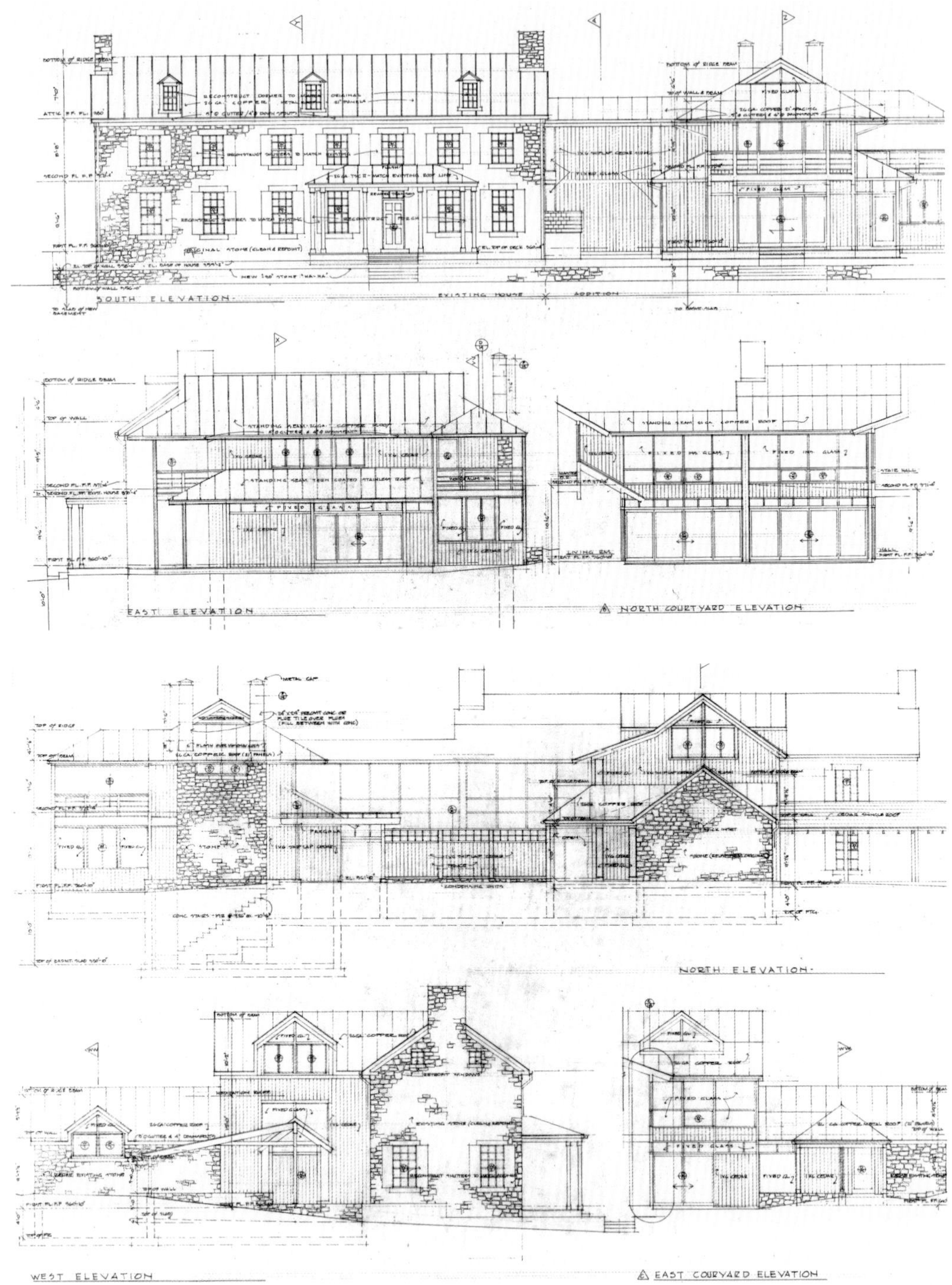

## *Architect*
# JAMES R. GRIEVES

PREPARING FOR THE DESIGN of the Tashiding house, we retained James R. "Jim" Grieves, FAIA, an esteemed architect based in Baltimore. A graduate of the University of Virginia, Jim earned his Master of Fine Arts in Architecture from Princeton University in the late 1950s, when Princeton's architecture school starred an international faculty that included William Shellman, Heath Licklider, Jean Labatut, and Enrico Peressutti.

Before founding his own firm, Jim gained invaluable design and management experience working for RTKL, a global architecture, planning, and design firm based in Annapolis and Baltimore. Subsequently, the firms of James R. Grieves Associates and Grieves, Worrall, Wright & O'Hatnick (GWWO) received dozens of national and regional awards for design and preservation, notably the Brandywine River Museum of Art, Baltimore Center Stage theater, the Grand Opera House in Wilmington, Delaware, a wing of the Walters Art Museum, Princeton University's Richardson Auditorium, and Everglades National Park Visitor Center, among others. ◆

OPPOSITE

*A view of the historical house from the driveway. This portion of the house represents slightly more than 25 percent of the completed structure, yet it is the dominant feature as one approaches the house.*

ABOVE

*From left, builder David Sutphen, superintendent Dale "Buck" Griffiths, and architect Jim Grieves consult during construction.*

Encouraged by Jim's assertion that he could work with the old house's structure to meet my objectives, I sought Tsognie's approval to purchase the property, which she did not give readily. She loved our Japanese-inspired house—in truth, it was difficult to imagine replicating the features and feel of our existing house after viewing the decrepit Western Run farmhouse. But once I agreed we would never sell our Monkton home, Tsognie acquiesced. Several days of negotiations later, just a week after first visiting the property, we successfully had it under contract.

Thus began a deliberate, multiyear design process. At Jim's request, we provided him with a thorough list of factors we wished him to consider as he undertook the initial schematic design. While many of these criteria centered around practical considerations—how many linear feet of bookshelves, the number of bedrooms and bathrooms, handicap accessibility, etc.—the overriding considerations dealt more with aesthetics, such as how the house should relate to its site rather than overpower it. We asked that the areas adjacent to the house, such as paved areas, walkways, fences, and walls, be extensions of the language of the house. We required that the design incorporate a space for a courtyard garden that could be viewed from as many rooms within the house as possible. Tsognie and I would take responsibility for the design and installation of that garden.

One thing we did not do was provide Jim with photographs of how the house should look. While we had definite views of how we wished to live in the house, we trusted Jim's creative and design skills to give it form. In the end, Jim was able to incorporate all our criteria into an elegant and harmonious plan.

When we purchased our Western Run Road property, the quarter-of-a-mile driveway led straight as an arrow from the road to the original house. Well before construction on the house began, at Jim's suggestion, we redirected the last hundred yards of the driveway so the house would be approached from an oblique angle. This would largely hide the proposed additions, which, when completed, would more than triple the square footage of the historical farmhouse. Balancing the old with the new and incorporating the existing features of the property with the new design were paramount. We wanted everything we did to form part of a unified whole.

We were fortunate to connect with an accomplished craft builder, David Sutphen of Southfen Residential Construction, who, with Jim's ongoing support and involvement, successfully undertook the construction of the house. The process took two and a half years.

ABOVE

*Looking southwest from the front of the house to the tree peonies and azaleas in bloom.*

OPPOSITE

*The stone walkway in front of the house after a dusting of snow.*

# RECONSTRUCTION *of the* HISTORIC FARMHOUSE

THE ORIGINAL 1818 portion of the limestone farmhouse presented severe structural problems. The rough-hewn logs that supported the floor had been set directly into the stone wall. The house had been constructed on a hill, so for almost two hundred years rainwater had settled against the north elevation of the house. The supporting logs had rotted as a result, some more than others, so the floors were far from level. A four-inch-high hump in the floor greeted visitors entering the front door. There was no insulation in any exterior wall.

Geotechnical borings around the house suggested that the constant flow of water had degraded the residual soils under the structure, thus exacerbating the settling. Remnants of the original wood shingle roof could be seen in the attic. At some point, a raised-seam tin roof had been installed over the shakes. When that roof failed, a previous owner had simply tarred over the tin. Three dormer windows had been installed in an earlier renovation, and, unfortunately, whoever installed them had cut through already undersized roof joists.

The front porch, also added at some later date, was decrepit and showed signs of imminent collapse. The unhappy reality was that without significant interventions the historic house was at the end of its useful life.

We decided to save the shell of the original house and construct a new space inside the historic walls. This was part of the larger project, which included substantial additions to the north and east of the existing farmhouse.

Stabilizing the walls of the historic house proved to be a complex and expensive undertaking, requiring no fewer than six separate steps. The first of these was a process called compact grouting, which used a rig similar to a well-drilling machine. A hollow pipe was driven into the soil until it hit bedrock, and then concrete was pumped through the pipe at great pressure to displace the surrounding soil. The process continued as the pipe was slowly removed; the result was a column of concrete that stabilized the soil under the walls of the house. Fifty such borings were made around the perimeter of the house. The deepest, at the northwest corner, went down fifty feet and took six cubic yards of concrete.

The second step involved underpinning, a process of hand digging and pouring a concrete footer under all walls where the foundation was insufficient or nonexistent.

LEFT

*The historical house covered in ivy, circa 1930.*

OPPOSITE

*The walls of the historical house during reconstruction.*

HomeWrap
SOUTHFEN

DEERE

HAYWARD BAKER

This had to be accomplished in three-foot sections to prevent the walls from collapsing.

In the third step, we completely regraded the area north of the house, removing the hill behind the structure and creating a swale and drainage system to divert water away from the house.

In the fourth step, the ruptured wall under the window on the west side of the house was carefully removed and the wall above braced, after which the wall was reconstructed.

The entire north wall of the 1818 house was excavated to below the stone foundation in the fifth step, to support the two-story wall. To accomplish this, an existing structure to the north of the house was carefully and permanently removed. The foundation of this part of the house was made of stacked stone and clay. There was no evidence of mortar in the wall. We raked out the clay from between the stones, and rebar was carefully worked through the wall, then wire mesh was attached to the rebar. Finally, the entire wall was covered in a thick layer (about a foot thick) of shotcrete, a process that involved spraying wet concrete under pressure out of a hose until all the fissures between the stones were filled and the additional thickness was achieved.

As we excavated for the additions to the north and west of the historical house, we discovered vast quantities of solid limestone. Paradoxically, we had unstable soil where we needed stone and stone where we hoped for unimpeded digging. In the sixth step, we spent weeks dynamiting stone. An unwanted side effect of this was that we opened springs, which continuously flowed into the excavated foundation hole. This required yet another "fix."

We overdug the foundation under the proposed basement, laid drainpipe in eighteen inches of gravel, then formed and poured the floor slab over the gravel. The constant flow of water was piped several hundred yards downhill to the lake, augmenting the springs that already fed the lake.

Years later, as we excavated the foundation for the pool pavilion, we ran into more springs. The solution was the same. The water was piped down the hill to connect with the earlier pipe, increasing the flow of water into the lake. Because this was pure spring water, we created a feature beside the lake where part of the water was diverted to flow through the mouth of a Japanese bronze dragon. The water that had created such problems now provides a refreshing drink on a hot day.

OPPOSITE, CLOCKWISE FROM TOP LEFT

*The original house prior to removing the roof; preparing to dynamite underground rock to the north side of the historical structure; prepping the wall before underpinning; applying shotcrete to the excavated north foundation; rebuilding the collapsing wall on the northwest corner of the house.*

ABOVE

*Springs under the house and pool pavilion feed the lake and offer a flow of cool, fresh water through a bronze dragon's mouth.*

FOLLOWING

*The house at night*

## The Courtyard Garden

During this period, Tsognie and I scoured the northern Baltimore County countryside, locating and purchasing the lichen- and moss-covered rocks and boulders that eventually formed much of the structure of the courtyard garden. An extraordinary gift of a collection of sixty- to eighty-year-old Kingsville boxwood was perfectly scaled to the garden we designed and installed as construction of the house neared completion. We introduced moss we gathered in flats from Emerald Hill then added several azaleas, ferns, and a Japanese maple to provide seasonal interest. The courtyard garden can only be viewed from within the house.

Several years passed before the moss knitted together in a natural way. Over time, the boxwood grew larger and embraced the garden's many rocks and boulders. Each morning, Tsognie sits on a mat facing the courtyard and enjoys her large mug of Lopchu flowery orange pekoe tea, a small luxury (she would say necessity) delivered regularly from the tea gardens of Darjeeling. And I know she thinks of Sikkim and all she misses from the land of her youth.

OPPOSITE
*The courtyard in autumn*

LEFT TOP
*Looking at the courtyard from within the house.*

LEFT BOTTOM
*Newly fallen snow in the courtyard garden.*

# House Interiors

RIGHT

*A stylized limestone carving of a Tibetan woman, sculpted by Baltimore artist Grace Turnbull, mid-twentieth century. On the floor sits a bronze Chinese dragon turtle, an important motif in Chinese feng shui.*

OPPOSITE

*A partial view of the entry gallery.*

FOLLOWING LEFT

*Looking north into the living room, which features an eclectic mix of furniture, including Chinese art deco chairs, a George Nakashima long table and coffee table, a Ming dynasty altar table, and two mid-century Niels Eilersen leather couches (only one visible).*

FOLLOWING RIGHT

*The two-story library*

THE JAPANESE PRINT
Its Evolution and Essence
IMPERIAL GARDENS OF JAPAN
THE GARDENS OF JAPAN
THE JAPANESE COURTYARD GARDEN
KATSURA VILLA
JAPANESE GARDENS

LEFT

*One of two dedicated art galleries in the residence, devoted primarily to Japanese painting and lacquer. On display is a six-panel botanical* byobo*, or folding screen, from the late 1920s.*

OPPOSITE

*The dining room features a self-portrait by son Palden Hamilton and a George Nakashima Persian walnut dining table with American walnut Conoid Chairs.*

PART TWO

# THE GARDENS

CHAPTER FOUR

# The Evolution of Tashiding

## *A Philosophy for Gardening*

PREVIOUS PAGE

*The wind disperses the prayers printed on Buddhist prayer flags placed on the western edge of the lake. Featured on the flags are depictions of Tibetan wind horses carrying symbols of Buddhist compassion and enlightenment.*

OPPOSITE & FOLLOWING

*The rock garden in the center of the driveway circle*

WHEN TSOGNIE AND I purchased the property we came to call Tashiding, we had no vision of how our land would evolve into the expansive garden that now exists—we saw it as a blank canvas, albeit a rather large one of thirty-five acres. We spent the first five years editing out dead and dying trees, removing miscellaneous junk, and clearing the many acres of invasive plants that had overtaken much of the property. Afterward, we began planting the first of more than a thousand trees and constructing berms and stone walls. We felt we needed to add interest to the parts of the property that were too flat and barren. Later, we purchased an adjoining sixty-five acres, made up mostly of forest. Improving the existing trail system and incorporating the trails into our original tract became our winter work.

We began the gardens several years before tackling the house, so there was no urgency to do something before it felt right. If you listen and observe carefully, the land speaks to you and suggests what it wants. The garden that exists today grew organically, over several decades, one step at a time.

Art is the imposing of a pattern on experience and our aesthetic enjoyment is recognition of the pattern.

—ALFRED NORTH WHITEHEAD

A trait we came to share with most of the community of garden creators we knew is that once we started, our motivation to do more only increased. For more than twenty years, we have continued to develop, expand, and refine our creation, limited only by property boundaries, energy, and financial considerations.

Unlike most people with gardens on the scale of Tashiding, we have never used a landscape architect or designer. From the beginning, we walked the property daily—and often individually rather than together. These walks allowed us to prioritize where to plant trees and construct stone walls, and consider how to make the silted-in farm pond a central feature.

## Marriage of East and West

Though the property's name and perhaps the garden itself suggest the exotic, I consider Tashiding to be the quintessential American garden. Though there are aspects that evoke Japan, Tashiding would look rather peculiar were it located in Japan, where garden design is bound by specific aesthetic principles. Nor is it a garden that one would create in mountainous Sikkim, where a relatively flat parcel of this size, should it even exist, would invariably be planted with crops. But Tashiding is right at home in the Maryland countryside.

# SPIRIT *of* PLACE

THERE ARE FUNDAMENTAL differences between "Eastern" and "Western" belief systems and aesthetics. In the West, for instance, a mountain is an inanimate object to be admired for its beauty or, for a mountaineer, to be conquered. By contrast, in Sikkim, as in much of Asia, almost every aspect of the natural world is imbued with its own divine-like power. In the Himalayan world, all things are interconnected. There is an animistic aspect to ancient trees, lakes, and the like. Sikkimese consider the land sacred, protected by spiritual deities on many levels.

Chief among these sacred places is Dzongna, or Kanchenjunga, the highest mountain in Sikkim and the world's third tallest at 28,169 feet. Every year, a ritual ceremony called Pang Lhabsol is held at Tsuklakhang, the royal chapel located in the capital of Gangtok. A monk in costume depicts Kanchenjunga as a wrathful, red-faced deity. In the presence of the masked Kanchenjunga, prominent lay citizens, colorfully dressed in ceremonial warrior costumes, perform elaborate dances to propitiate Kanchenjunga and invoke him to continue to bless and protect both the country and the Buddhist Dharma (the holy tenets that form the core of Buddhist practice).

BELOW, LEFT TO RIGHT
*Warrior dancers; the masked "Kanchenjunga"; warrior dancers performing.*

OPPOSITE
*Kanchenjunga, whose five peaks, according to Sikkimese lore, represent the "five treasures of the eternal snows." The treasures are gold, silver, gems, grain, and Buddhist religious texts.*

# TSOGNIE'S MEDITATION *on* TASHIDING

MOST MORNINGS, I wake early to mist rising on the lake and ready myself for a morning walk. In prayerful meditation, I move along the trails that meander through the woods and lead to the steep steps down into the stream valley. Sights along the way too often lead my mind astray but I am pulled back to meditation when I arrive at the tranquil valley, where I imagine I hear the murmuring prayers of monks on their descent down the hill.

Autumn, with its crisp, cool air, is my favorite season. My mother tells me it is the start of the eighth month of the Tibetan calendar, when the cleansing rains come. Autumn marks the time when the hermit monks and yogis complete their meditation and descend from the mountains. I am happy for the rains and the blessings they bring.

Seasonal change is subtle in the house's courtyard garden compared with the transformation I observe in the forest. When I return from my walk, I sit contentedly with my tea, chatting on a video call with my mother in Sikkim. She draws comfort from the knowledge that we are connected by the symbolic cultural ties Douglas and I have embedded throughout the property: the ritual prayer for blessings buried in the foundations of our house, the courtyard garden reflecting the protection of the guardian mountains of Sikkim, and the prayer flags that flutter all around the grounds. I recall the early years when I resisted the move here. It seemed impossible that Douglas could create a second place where we would feel at home in America. The Japanese house in the woods in Monkton, sanctified and blessed by the highest Nyingma Rinpoche, was "home" to us.

Eventually, Douglas won me over with his enthusiasm for his grand new plan. Lured into walking acres of nurseries in search of specimen plants and trees, driving round the countryside looking for the perfect rocks, I was hooked. We worked hard to recreate the sacred ground so essential for our spiritual growth.

Preparing for this book on the gardens has made me aware of how enormous a task we have taken on. Each new garden project fueled Douglas's creative juices and led to another. As he took off further afield, I concentrated on little projects, weeding moss in the courtyard or creating space for bulbs and shrubs we liked. Uncovering the natural beauty along the tree line and streambeds, I was mostly on my hands and knees looking down, lost in the world of minutiae. Douglas crafted up and out. Being pulled into the book project has made me look up and acknowledge how successfully he has grown a rich environment in which the body, mind, and spirit can move and meld. Gone is my initial thought of exile, as if to the plains of India; Douglas has grown hills and green forest reminiscent of my beloved Himalayan homeland. Tashiding, wellspring of auspiciousness indeed.

OPPOSITE, CLOCKWISE FROM TOP LEFT
*Hydrangeas, a hellebore, lilies, and another hellebore, all among Tsognie's favorites.*

ABOVE
*The intense purple of a grape hyacinth*

One cannot enter our driveway without noticing the many Far Eastern influences that exist throughout the property. Rows of Himalayan Buddhist prayer flags located beside the lake and above stone walls catch the wind, distributing the printed prayers for the benefit of all sentient beings. Dozens of vintage and antique Japanese granite lanterns and pagodas add a spiritual dimension and mark places to stop and reflect or perhaps change direction. At the same time, it is not the identifiable Eastern details that give Tashiding an Asian feel, but rather its underlying sensibility.

## The Landscape Develops

Looking back, I recognize influences relating to the garden's development that I understood intuitively but never considered part of a conscious design philosophy. Other than the house and its immediate environs, which are rectilinear, almost every other feature of our garden is either curved or part of a random pattern. Straight lines are rare in nature. But most Western gardens feature straight lines, geometric forms and shapes, and neat rows of plants and trees, all of which highlight the mastery of the designer. There is an order that reflects a certain primacy.

In our garden, the primary intent is to blend all the garden elements into a natural-looking landscape. While we strive for beauty, the overriding consideration is the way we or our visitors feel in the garden. Walking the grounds gives one a sense of being part of something rather than just an observer of a creation that is separate and apart.

Naturalist John Muir once observed, "Of all the paths you take in life, make sure a few are dirt." It is noteworthy that Muir spoke of the path rather than a destination. Our forest and gardens have miles of paths, most of them dirt.

The occasional conflicts Tsognie and I have usually involve my desire to impose a measure of order over aspects of the garden, areas in the landscape where I want things to look a certain way. In the overall scheme of things, our disagreements are minor, but they do at times reflect differing East-West perspectives.

I am quick to replace a failing tree that, in my view, mars the landscape. Tsognie will want it to live out its life, however sad and decrepit it may look. When two specimens encroach on each other, I typically want to remove one to save the other.

ABOVE
*Bluets, or Quaker ladies, introduced in the courtyard garden as stowaways in the flats of moss we transported from Emerald Hill, my childhood home.*

OPPOSITE
*Looking west past the lake and prayer flags to a granite Japanese lantern in the distance*

Tsognie loves both her "children" equally, whatever handicap may develop. I shear our many boxwoods to varying degrees, borrowing from Japanese garden practice, in order to create and maintain a pleasing composition, while Tsognie finds such activity unnatural, perhaps too contrived.

In developing Tashiding, we have been motivated by our desire to surround ourselves with an environment that invites a sense of harmony and well-being. Our property is part arboretum, part park, and indeed, as my Scottish mother often teased, part Xanadu. It is a garden for both walking and quiet contemplation, for feeling the thrill of the wind on a cool October or March day, or for sitting in the teahouse on a rainy afternoon, watching the wind form abstract ripples on the surface of the lake.

As I reflect on our creation, I recognize themes more commonly associated with music or literature: a sense of joy and expectation, of longing and melancholia, of decay and the promise of renewal and rebirth. It is truly a garden for spring, summer, autumn, and winter as well as the seasons of a person's life.

The process of planting, building the various elements, and performing ongoing maintenance is as important as the garden itself. We are reminded of the Chinese Zen koan:

Before enlightenment,
Chop wood, carry water.
After enlightenment,
Chop wood, carry water.

When we first began to arrange and plant the thousands of trees, shrubs, and other plant material, we could easily see our hand in all we did. As the years pass, however, each tree and garden plant grows in its own unique way, knitting together to form a new and perhaps more naturalistic landscape. It is increasingly apparent that we haven't forced our will upon the land; rather, Mother Nature has reclaimed her domain. Our involvement is perhaps not appreciably different from the bird, the insect, or the wind that carries the seed to new and fertile soil. We are part of the larger plan, not its master.

The process is not unlike giving birth to children, setting the foundation for their lives, then watching as they take their own form as adults. It is one of the many joys of contributing to an environment we hope will in turn shape the lives of our family's future generations.

PREVIOUS PAGES
*Autumn and winter views just west of the lake, with a snow viewing lantern, or* yukimi-gata, *in the foreground.*

OPPOSITE
*A Seiryu Japanese maple shows off its deep red autumnal color at the northwest corner of the lake.*

CHAPTER FIVE

# Elements of the Garden

## *Structure, Texture, Color & Seasonal Change*

OPPOSITE

*Reflections of conifers and deciduous trees, including an old apple tree, play across the surface of the lake.*

MARYLAND ENJOYS FOUR distinct seasons. Summers are hot and humid, with temperatures reaching the mid- to high nineties Fahrenheit. Winters are cold, with nighttime temperatures often dipping into the teens and sometimes single digits. Snowfall tends to be erratic, with total winter accumulations ranging from five or six inches to more than fifty. Yearly rainfall approaches forty-five inches, distributed nearly equally across all twelve months.

Creating a garden with four-season interest challenged us to consider our property holistically. We wanted the entirety of the gardens, including all the hardscape and plant material, to be experienced as a unified whole. One way we accomplished this was to repeat design elements such as stone lanterns and favorite tree species throughout the property. We also took care to create natural transitions between the different areas of the garden, always bearing in mind our experience of the gardens throughout the year.

# Stonework

To date, we have constructed approximately 1,000 linear feet of stone walls. Because the historical stone house was built of limestone quarried on the property, we decided that walls adjoining or behind the house and in proximity to the nearby pool should be constructed of the same stone.

Walls around the lake and the peony pavilion, near the stream, or in areas delineating elevation changes are of a different, darker stone. We enlisted the help of a local farmer, Matt Sauter, who was familiar with properties in western Baltimore County, to locate, acquire, and deliver vast quantities of this indigenous granite from old dry-stacked stone walls found at the edge of agricultural fields. This fieldstone cannot be shaped by chisel and hammer—it tends to shatter—so it must be laid in a wall like the pieces of a jigsaw puzzle. The very trait that makes it hard to work with, however, yields a result with the character of a two-hundred-year-old wall. Bits of moss and lichen, which might take decades to establish, are often in evidence.

With the help of stone contractor Andreas Grothe, we were also able to purchase hundreds of linear feet of granite curbing and thousands of Belgian blocks reclaimed from Baltimore City streets. Much of this material was found in an overgrown "stone graveyard" located near the Baltimore zoo in an isolated area of the city's renowned Druid Hill Park. Interestingly, this treasure trove of abandoned stone was located next to the area where zoo personnel dump elephant dung removed from the zoo's elephant compound.

One advantage of repurposing old stone is that it possesses the patina of age. No two pieces of the granite curbing are alike, and the irregularity of the pieces gives a rustic feel when they are used for paths or steps. For larger projects, such as the stone steps leading from the stream valley to the top of the ridge, we imported cut stone nearly identical in color to the older granite curbing. We often mix old and new together—there is beauty in both the combination and the imperfection—but we make sure that all of the material we bring in blends in color and texture with the native boulders and rock outcroppings found throughout Tashiding.

Many popular English-language books on Japanese gardening or aesthetics include interpretive musings on the symbolic nature of every rock, plant, flower, and pebble. This information is often overblown and embellished: sometimes, a rock is just a rock. There are rules of aesthetics that apply to the creation of Japanese gardens, but they deal

more with how rocks, plants, pathways, and water are used to create harmonious and balanced designs. Gardens in Zen temples often include groupings of carefully selected rocks surrounded by moss and a sea of fine gravel. In their spareness and abstraction, they invite each viewer to seek a personal interpretation.

That is not to say that there are no connections between Buddhist practice and the objects that have found their way into the Tashiding landscape. We maintain numerous Himalayan Buddhist prayer flags that disperse blessings throughout the land when the wind blows. Though the flags are printed on white cloth, tabs in five different colors are sewn along the edge of each flag. These represent the five elements of Buddhist cosmology, beginning with yellow, closest to the ground and representing the earth, followed by green (water), red (fire), white (air and wind), and, on the top, blue (sky). Balancing these elements, in the Buddhist belief system, creates environmental harmony as well as accord between the body and the mind.

PREVIOUS PAGE
*A partial view of the peony pavilion*

RIGHT
*A swale, located just south of the house, used to control rainwater runoff.*

OPPOSITE
*Rustic sculptures of sheep observe a row of prayer flags, an important feature of Himalayan Buddhism.*

# Antique Japanese Lanterns

For several decades, we have collected vintage and antique Japanese stone lanterns and pagodas. The thirty or so in our collection are dispersed throughout the property. Some are integrated with installations of boulders and plant material; others rest next to the lake or mark places of particular interest.

Stone lanterns were originally used to light pathways to Japanese Buddhist and Shinto temples. During the sixteenth century, Japanese tea masters began to incorporate lanterns into gardens as decorative elements. Their presence in our garden contributes to the subtle spiritual atmosphere many visitors experience.

The five distinct elements of traditional Japanese stone lanterns echo the symbolism of the prayer flags. The bottom piece, which touches the ground, represents the earth. The next section represents water followed by one representing fire, with the two topmost sections pointing upward and representing air and the sky. The similar symbolism of the prayer flags and lanterns in our garden was not planned but rather an act of serendipity.

Our collection also includes a selection of Japanese bronze lanterns, which were originally designed to hang from the eaves of temples. Many of these we have electrified and suspended from custom-designed posts, especially around the perimeter of the pool area, where they cast a comforting glow after nightfall.

Others are hung on long copper chains from the upper branches of the three large sycamore trees that grow in front of the house. Here, we have interspersed bronze wind bells among the lanterns. Both the bells and the lanterns have strong associations with the Buddhist world: the sound of the bells reminds us to be mindful in all we do.

## Berms and Mounds

When Tsognie first stood on the porch of the historic house in 1998 and looked south across the relatively flat landscape of fields and pasture, she said, "It looks like the plains of India," displeased by the flatness of the landscape. I recalled, during Tsognie's first trip to the States years earlier, describing my home state of Maryland as "America in miniature," noting that we had bays and rivers, rolling hills, flat agricultural land, and mountains. She perked up when I said "mountains." Shortly after, I took her on a road trip to the Appalachian Mountains of Western Maryland. After driving for several hours, I announced that we had arrived at our destination. "Where are the mountains?" she asked, looking around. "We are on top of one," I responded as we sat atop a three-thousand-foot peak. Her disappointment was palpable. In Sikkim, foothills rise to elevations of up to ten thousand feet. In Tsognie's world, mountains are snow-clad massifs that rise high above in every direction.

Obviously, one cannot turn a field into a mountain, or even a foothill. But by constructing elevated islands of plantings in what had been open pasture, we have created vistas that suggest greater elevation changes than actually exist. In places, these islands limit or block views in certain directions in ways that frame others. Almost all these landscaped islands share similar plantings, so they feel as if they are part of a unified whole. They also serve as counterpoints to the rocky island in the lake, though they exist in a sea of lawn rather than water.

RIGHT

*Mounding Korean boxwoods (*Buxus microphylla *var.* koreana*) adjoin the peony pavilion and help frame the view of the house, located further up the hill.*

OPPOSITE

*In the maple and conifer garden, we used mounded soil, a collection of large rocks, and a mix of plant material to create a painterly effect.*

# Trees

In one sense, Tashiding is a collection of trees, both deciduous and coniferous. Though we have limited the palette of stone and bronze elements in the gardens, we have done the opposite with trees and other plant material, building a diverse collection of deciduous and coniferous trees of different sizes, textures, shapes, and hues.

The meadow and open pastureland west of the stream offer a good example. Aside from a row of indigenous cherry and mulberry trees that grew along what was once a fence line, the area was flat and largely open when we purchased the property. Western Run Road runs along the southern edge of the pasture, allowing for an open view all the way to the house, which was set back from the road about 1,200 feet.

We began by visiting nurseries and selecting trees that appealed to us, then planted them in ways that created vistas from multiple directions. We didn't set out to create an arboretum, though our collector tendencies quickly took over. We began to juxtapose deciduous trees with conifers, conscious of creating enough space between trees so each had room to take its own form without hindrance. There are hundreds of tree species that do well in our mid-Atlantic climate. We wanted examples of as many as our space would allow. The result is a lovely meadow that provides shade, habitat, and food for a wide variety of birds, as well as visual and seasonal interest. The space doesn't give the impression of being planned in advance, because, of course, it wasn't.

We have planted certain types of trees in drifts, as others plant bulbs or perennials. In order to tie the entire property together, we dispersed many specimens of the same tree throughout the property. For example, we have planted groups of dawn redwoods in five different areas of our expansive acreage. We have approximately one hundred Japanese maples placed throughout the garden. These are often planted in slightly elevated positions juxtaposed with dwarf conifers, boxwoods, and ground covers. The diverse plant community provides contrasting structure, color, and texture in all seasons.

Tashiding reminds us of places far away and of my Maryland roots. Each tree we plant has a unique fragrance: this is true of both flowering and nonflowering ones, as the scents emanate from leaves and needles as much as from blooms. These scents change with the seasons. Mixing varieties of trees together in one place is like blending perfume, subtle but distinct.

One impulse from a vernal wood
May teach you more of man,
Of moral evil and of good,
Than all the sages can.

—WILLIAM WORDSWORTH

## Marrying the Existing Forest with the Garden

Japanese gardeners often use the term "borrowed scenery" to describe how adjoining or distant landscapes are used as part of an overall garden design. In our case, we wanted to soften the transition between the established forest and the plantings and other elements we introduced. We worked to achieve a natural flow, in part by creating grassy areas that gradually narrow into moss-covered paths leading farther into the denser forest. Walking paths adjoin the stream on both sides, past natural stone outcroppings, as well as stone paths we constructed and set amid existing large, moss-covered boulders. Each stop along the path invites the visitor to enjoy an intimate experience while at the same time encouraging further exploration. In the forested valley adjoining the path, we planted numerous Japanese maples as understory trees, enhancing the feel that all areas of the greater property are connected to one another.

RIGHT
*Stone steps leading from the valley to the ridge above.*

OPPOSITE
*Elevated view of the gate and stepping stones along the stream.*

## The Seasons

Beginning in April and running into June, every deciduous tree puts forth a flush of new leaves; perennials rise from winter's obscurity to display spring foliage and flowers; coniferous trees push up candles of new growth, accompanied by purplish and green pinecones. Flowering magnolias and the apples, peaches, and cherries in our orchard bloom, tempting a mid-spring frost—a challenge that often ends in disappointment.

The many varieties of birds that populate Tashiding's trees herald the new season with a euphony of song beginning just before sunrise. Our peacocks, their feathers now in full form, become more animated. Their cries punctuate the night, evoking the romantic night strolls Tsognie and I took in the Lodi Gardens of New Delhi decades earlier. Tree frogs and toads emerge from their winter hibernation to gather in large numbers in the wetlands that border our stream. The sounds of croaking and trilling signal the beginning of mating season.

In early June through mid-July, the tangle of invasive multiflora rose and honeysuckle that bury our neighbors' neglected fence lines releases the most sublime fragrance, particularly at dusk, accompanied by scores of newly emerged fireflies that hover and flicker just above the meadows and hayfield.

In late summer, many plants begin to show the effects of dry and hot weather. Native walnut trees start to drop their yellowing leaves, and the Joe Pye weed, milkweed, and butterfly bushes that edge the lake begin to bloom, attracting a profusion of insects, including bees and hundreds of yellow and black swallowtails as well as beloved orange and black monarch butterflies just arrived after overwintering in Mexico.

As late summer heat yields to cooler nights, the many deciduous trees in our forest and park (and especially the many Japanese maples) begin to display their fall foliage in hues of amber and yellow, auburn and purple, crimson red and burnt umber. Just as we welcomed the late spring and summer heat that followed winter, we now embrace the cooler weather that is the harbinger of winter ahead.

As temperatures fall and days grow shorter, the bare branches of deciduous trees take center stage. The exfoliating white bark on the high branches of our giant sycamores appears luminescent against a backdrop of deep blue late-autumn and winter sky. The Japanese maples, beautiful in every season, display the complexity of their branching structure, looking like well-tended Japanese bonsai.

Starting in mid-December we begin to anticipate snow, though white Christmases in Maryland are rare. Our sleds are brought out of storage; their use is eagerly anticipated by our granddaughters. Any time of year, but particularly in fall, winter, and spring, we take long hikes on the several miles of trails that meander through Tashiding's forest. For us, snow, rain, and sleet are perfect weather for a walk. Perhaps those are the conditions that most remind us of the forests and mountains of the central Himalayas. In recent years, the Japanese have given a name—*shinrin-yoku*—to the beneficial practice of "forest bathing." But make no mistake, we are warmly wrapped up, as my Scottish mother would often remark, "like a clootie dumpling."

March is a transition month. We often observe that, "March comes in like a lion and goes out like a lamb," but it is not unusual for us to have frosts as late as May 10, so planting vegetables before that date can be a bit risky.

And thus, the cycle begins anew. We are a year older, all the trees are more mature, and we are ready again to get our hands in the soil.

CHAPTER SIX

# Walking the Gardens

## *Experiential Landscapes*

OPPOSITE

*The sky is a borrowed element in this landscape composition of form, color, and texture. In autumn, the decaying leaves of the weeping katsura tree to the left emit a sweet fragrance similar to that of the cotton candy we enjoyed as children.*

WE GIVE ONE PIECE OF ADVICE to Tashiding's visitors: wear good walking shoes! Ours is an expansive garden. From the house, there are no obvious paths or routes that lead in any direction, though the front lawns flow toward the lake and beyond.

Some have noted that walking the property is akin to following the course of a meandering river. On our daily walks, Tsognie and I seldom follow the same route twice in a row. In the heat of the summer, Tsognie might prefer the shade and lower temperatures found in the stream valley. We have never cancelled a garden tour or event because of rain: damp conditions seem to enhance the fragrance emitted by the soil and myriad trees and shrubs.

This chapter presents the garden through all four seasons. Though by necessity we have sequenced broad sections of the garden for clarity, no part of the garden stands alone; rather, each part draws on the visual and thematic elements of adjoining areas.

# A GARDENER'S WALK

On my daily walks through the garden and forest, I occasionally stop to use my iPhone to record something that interests me. These are quick snapshots, often of a fleeting moment, that reflect the simple beauty that seems to exist everywhere, in things both large and small.

## The Lake, Teahouse, and Meadow

ONE CANNOT OVERSTATE the importance of the lake to the overall aesthetic enjoyment and appearance of the garden. On bright summer days, blue sky and billowing white clouds are reflected on the surface of the water, affirming the connection between earth and sky. Even a slight breeze creates ripples that reflect shimmering sunlight throughout the day; at night, the movement of the moon across the sky is mirrored on the lake's dark surface.

Plants that like wet feet flourish in the shallow water and saturated soil at lake's edge. In mid- to late spring, thousands of yellow flag irises bloom. We have interspersed Siberian and Japanese irises of different hues, creating blue, white, yellow, and purple blooms to contrast with the sea of yellow.

The water attracts a wide variety of birds. Regular visitors include great blue herons, green herons, kingfishers, barn swallows, and mallards. Each spring, and at intervals during the summer, a lone osprey hunts on the lake, trying without success to catch one of our Japanese koi, who sense the danger and stay deep underwater. On rare occasions we have seen snowy egrets and cormorants.

The Japanese-influenced teahouse, complete with tatami mats, provides refuge in rough weather and is a wonderful retreat for listening to music while reading a book and sipping a glass of wine. In the winter, a small heater keeps the interior temperature at a comfortable seventy-two degrees. In the summer, the veranda is a convenient place to stay out of the sun while feeding the resident koi and painted turtles that quickly gather around when they hear a stone rapping on the deck.

OPPOSITE

*Looking south toward the teahouse, yellow flag irises in full bloom on the western shore of the lake. These irises usually bloom in time for Tsognie's birthday in late May.*

OPPOSITE
*In a contrast of textures, a moss-covered boulder rises from a sea of juniper and is framed by a red Japanese maple.*

ABOVE LEFT
*A river rock cairn assembled by our granddaughters sits atop a boulder on the northwest corner of the lake. Cairns are often constructed on mountain paths as spiritual tokens.*

ABOVE RIGHT
*The simple beauty of a paperbark maple's exfoliating bark.*

# REIMAGINING *the* LAKE

ASIDE FROM THE HOUSE, the lake was the largest and most complex single project we undertook. Originally constructed in the 1920s, the lake, particularly the northern half, had significant accumulations of silt, so that in places the water depth could be measured in inches. We pumped about half the water out of the lake and spent weeks dredging and hauling silt out of the northern portion until we reached the original depth of about four or five feet. We spread the removed muck in a nearby field to dry out, which took about a year. We then trucked that soil to a spot just beyond the southwest corner of the lake to form a substantial berm, on which we planted a variety of maples, pines, and other specimen trees and shrubs.

Having restored the northern half of the lake to its original depth, we lined the affected area with heavy landscape fabric, which we covered with more than 1,000 tons of Delaware river rock. We extended the river rock beyond the confines of the lake, creating a rocky beach area.

At the northernmost corner of the lake, and extending westward to the newly created rocky beach, we constructed hundreds of linear feet of thirty-inch-high stone walls where the edges of the lake had been damaged by years of animal intrusion. In the shallow water near the wall, we installed more landscape fabric and several hundred tons of the same river rock. Just beyond that shelf, the lake quickly deepened to a channel about nine feet deep. When rainfall and natural springs refilled the lake, the stone wall was about two-thirds underwater, creating a clean edge.

The basic structure of the island in the lake was created during this time, though it would take years of transporting rocks and plant material by raft to create the island that exists today.

BELOW, LEFT TO RIGHT
*Recontouring the field on the northwest corner of the lake; our collection of rocks and granite Belgian blocks awaiting placement; constructing the stone wall that defines the western edge of the lake after dredging was completed.*

OPPOSITE
*Fresh spring water from beneath the house flows into the lake through the mouth of an antique bronze Japanese temple dragon.*

LEFT & OPPOSITE
*Two views of the island in the lake. Most of the rocks on the island were floated out on a raft and positioned by hand.*

OPPOSITE

*A fog rises from the still waters of the lake on a winter's day.*

RIGHT

*View north toward the peony pavilion; the fall color of a willow oak is reflected in the lake. The playhouse is just visible in the top left corner of the photograph.*

FOLLOWING

*A winter snow squall coats all in a sea of white.*

PREVIOUS PAGE

*Under the teahouse eave, a rain chain adds a decorative element in lieu of a downspout. An electrified antique Japanese lantern is one of many we have repurposed throughout the property.*

OPPOSITE

*Although supported by an elaborate underwater infrastructure, the teahouse seems to float on the lake.*

RIGHT

*Japanese tatami mats and a low ceiling invite guests to sit inside the teahouse. The moon window is a distinctive element, repeated in the peony and pool pavilions and the playhouse.*

OPPOSITE

*Joe Pye weed proliferates around the lake. From mid- to late summer it blooms, attracting numerous butterflies, including this female swallowtail, identified as such by the blue color on its hind wings. In summer, the lake teems with life, including purplish and yellow irises around the edges and swirling Japanese koi in deeper water.*

RIGHT

*Red cones on a spruce tree to the west of the lake provide natural ornament.*

LEFT

*Midsummer peaches in our small orchard. Picked right off the tree, they're a favorite snack on garden walks.*

OPPOSITE

*Dawn redwoods in the west meadow in their autumnal raiment.*

FOLLOWING LEFT

*Raised mounds and trees on a foggy summer morning in the west meadow.*

FOLLOWING RIGHT

*A plein air oil painting of part of the west meadow, looking south toward Western Run Road, by Palden Hamilton.*

## The Conifer and Maple Garden and Hayfield

ONE OF TSOGNIE'S GREAT garden successes was locating a cache of very large rocks on our friends' property at the other end of Western Run Valley. She approached the owners, who generously told her she could have them, providing, of course, that she would move them.

This task was more complicated than it would seem—the two largest weighed 23,000 pounds each. To the rescue came Andreas Grothe, who had helped us locate and move so much of our rock material. We rented a large crane and, under the supervision of Andreas, were able to load them on his large flatbed truck and deliver them to Tashiding. After the rocks were set in place, the basic structure of the conifer and maple garden was established. We mounded soil around the rocks to create a bit of elevation change, then over time planted a variety of conifers, including a golden hinoki cypress, a Tanyosho pine, and a mix of mugo pines, Korean boxwoods, and junipers. We planted a couple of cutleaf Japanese maples among the conifers to add contrasting texture and seasonal color.

Tsognie was also able to purchase two large bronze giraffes, which graze nearby in a small grove of walnut and mulberry trees. Their inclusion in the garden delights children and adults alike.

Every Labor Day weekend, the hayfield becomes an archery range for our annual Bhutanese archery tournament. Overlooking the range are five stone reproduction Chinese Qin warriors mounted on a large, rectangular stone plinth. When the hay in the field is high, obscuring the plinth, the warriors seem to float as if they are not connected to the ground in any way.

Clouds are hills in vapour,
hills are clouds in stone,—
a phantasy in time's dream.

—RABINDRANATH TAGORE

OPPOSITE
*Lime green Japanese maple leaves appear to glow, set off by hot pink azaleas.*

ABOVE LEFT & RIGHT
*Throughout the garden, a variety of Japanese maples lend vibrant color that changes with the seasons.*

LEFT

*Each spring, we allow the hay to grow to full height before it is cut, raked, and baled. By mid-June, we begin to mow and groom the field in preparation for the Bhutanese archery tournament we host each Labor Day weekend.*

OPPOSITE

*In a nod to whimsy, two bronze giraffes graze at the edge of the field in a small grove of native walnut and mulberry trees.*

FOLLOWING

*Reproduction stone Qin warriors, modeled after the famed terra-cotta warriors in Xi'an, China, seem to float above the hayfield.*

It is as solitary where I live as
on the prairies. It is as much
Asia or Africa as New England.
I have, as it were, my own
sun and moon and stars, and
a little world all to myself.

—HENRY DAVID THOREAU

# The Pool, Aviary, and Playhouse

DURING THE SUMMER, the pool and pool pavilion become the center of activity. We've read surveys of children visiting Disney World that asked their favorite part of their vacation; the number one answer was the hotel pool. We are not surprised. On a hot summer day, people gravitate to water. Our pool is designed to appeal to all ages. There are two twenty-meter lap lanes, a large circular shallow end ranging from four to five feet deep, a long infinity edge, and a foot-deep "tanning ledge," popular with adults in chairs and very small children. In the deep end, a large slab of granite serves as a diving or jumping rock.

The pool pavilion includes a bathroom, an outdoor shower with a privacy fence, and cooking facilities.

Just up the hill from the pool area is the aviary, populated with peacocks and red golden pheasants. Collecting the peacock and pheasant feathers in late summer and early autumn, when the birds molt, is a favorite activity of my granddaughters.

Further along the tree line, and set back up the hill, is the children's playhouse, which Tsognie likes to call "Granddad's folly." Something of an entertainment complex, this area includes a seventeen-foot-high tube slide and a twenty-foot swinging bridge that leads to the playhouse. The large interior includes two built-in sleeping platforms, each located in front of a moon window, as well as a queen-size bed. In the winter, a small electric heater keeps the interior at a comfortable level. Both the pool house and the playhouse were collaborations with architect Jim Grieves.

OPPOSITE
*Two Japanese copper* shachihoko *flank the walkway that leads from the house to the pool.* Shachihoko *are mythical Chinese and Japanese creatures who, as a reward for their perseverance in reaching the farthest point upriver, are transformed from carp into dragons. Depicted at the moment of metamorphosis, they have a dragon's head and a fish's body. In Japan, they are often mounted on roofs, where they are thought to protect buildings from fire.*

FOLLOWING LEFT
*The view looking south from behind and above the house and the pool area.*

FOLLOWING RIGHT
*Reclaimed and repurposed architectural elements, including stone millstones topped by a Japanese copper finial, and stone and copper lanterns.*

OPPOSITE, CLOCKWISE FROM TOP LEFT

*Close-up views of summer-blooming lilies; black-eyed Susans, Maryland's state flower; decorative Japanese bronze geese, symbols of love and devotion; hydrangeas.*

RIGHT

*The steps leading from the pool area toward the aviary.*

FOLLOWING PAGES

*The pool and pool pavilion. Note the crab lifeguard chair near the diving rock. Blue crabs steamed in Old Bay Seasoning are a Maryland delicacy that we always serve on Independence Day weekend, which is capped off with a fireworks display.*

PREVIOUS PAGES

*The view from the pool area looking up the hill toward the aviary.*

LEFT

*Another view of the aviary, from the terraced lawn next to the house.*

OPPOSITE

*The stone and river rock landing above the pool area. Here, quarried granite boulders surrounded by shorn boxwoods flank recycled granite curbing steps. In the flat landing, cut granite rests in a bed of natural flat river rock. Fragrant creeping thyme fills the spaces between the steps.*

OPPOSITE

*Another view of the landing. The shorn boxwoods contrast nicely with the specimen red Japanese maple, which adds a sense of enclosure.*

RIGHT

*A bald-faced hornet nest, certainly a wonder of nature, grows safely in a Satyr Hill holly between the house and the pool.*

LEFT

*An India Blue peafowl, or peacock, rests on a locust branch in the aviary. Certainly one of the most extraordinarily beautiful birds in the world, peafowl require little care and can withstand the heat of summer as well as the cold of Maryland winters.*

OPPOSITE & FOLLOWING

*The aviary in winter. To the right of the main aviary is a connected structure that enables our red golden pheasants and peafowl to get out of the wind.*

OPPOSITE

*Every child and teen needs a "safe" place to escape adults and dwell in the world of their imagination.*

RIGHT

*The seventeen-foot-high tube slide is popular with children and adults alike.*

OPPOSITE

*The rope bridge leading from the tube slide tower to the playhouse.*

ABOVE LEFT

*A Bavarian wood gnome mounted on a tree welcomes all to the steps leading up to the slide and playhouse.*

ABOVE RIGHT

*The interior of the playhouse features two built-in single beds, each in front of a moon window, as well as a queen-size bed.*

# The Peony Pavilion

MY MOTHER, MARGARET, died unexpectedly at age seventy-seven in December of 2006. Just weeks before her death, at my suggestion, my parents had agreed to build a house on our property so we could be together as a family through the end of their lives. Sadly, this was not to be. As soon as Mother entered the hospital, several weeks before her passing, she fell into a coma from which she never regained consciousness. My father moved in with us while she was in the hospital.

Mother never had the opportunity to say goodbye to those she loved or to make a last wish. But she and I were kindred spirits; I knew her last wish would be that we take care of her husband of fifty-seven years, knowing her death would be devastating to him. Subsequently, Dad never left our home, spending his last eight years surrounded by loving family and friends.

I decided to build a special place on the property where I could sit quietly, surrounded by flowers Mother loved, in quiet contemplation of her life and the many contributions she made to mine. In 2012, architect Jim Grieves and I collaborated on the design of a structure we came to call the peony pavilion, after one of Mother's favorite flowers. We designed a central roofed structure with rose arbors extending in two directions. In addition to tree peonies and roses, we planted hellebores and irises, with a mass of Korean boxwood grown in undulating mounds to the west of the pavilion. To the east, we constructed a rock garden similar to the house's courtyard garden.

Mother's ultimate compliment was to refer to a special person as a "peach." It seemed more than coincidence that a Japanese granite lantern with a relief of a peach became available. It is installed in the most prominent place in the peony pavilion rock garden.

OPPOSITE
*Looking south past the peony pavilion to the lake.*

FOLLOWING
*A spring view from below the peony pavilion looking toward the house. Roses, climbing hydrangeas, and tree peonies are all in bloom.*

## The Stone Bridge, Shrine, and Stream

THE STREAM AT TASHIDING splits our original thirty-five acres from north to south, with approximately 85 percent of the property falling west of the stream. But the 15 percent that lies east of the stream is no less important to the garden than the larger tract.

Accessing the eastern portion requires crossing the stream, which was originally not possible unless one was willing to suffer wet feet or wear high waterproof boots. To solve this problem, we installed several bridges, the northernmost one located approximately one hundred feet from the peony pavilion.

This simple bridge is a single piece of granite that spans twenty feet and rests on stone piers located on each side of the stream. The impressive slab of granite, which weighs more than five tons, was once part of a set of steps to a now-demolished city building in Baltimore.

This bridge, and the stream beneath it, is a center of activity for our granddaughters and wildlife alike. The girls enjoy playing in the water under and near the bridge, often catching then releasing the minnows and crayfish that congregate there. These same aquatic creatures attract herons, kingfishers, and raccoons, for whom they represent a tasty meal.

Directly across from the bridge is a large rock face, adorned in moss and shaded by a small grove of ironwood trees. This marks the beginning of a dramatic departure from the generally flat terrain of the meadow. The land quickly tilts upward, forming the southern flank of the ridge that delineates the Western Run Valley from the Belfast Valley to the north.

Just along the trail that leads north, paralleling the stream, is the berm of a pond that no longer exists. The meander of the stream long ago eroded the western bank: large concrete slabs, mostly buried, suggest this was probably part of a simple water-powered mill at some point in the farm's history. On top of the existing berm, we installed an old Japanese Shinto structure we converted into a Buddhist shrine.

Growing in the stream nearby is a large colony of watercress, which Tsognie regularly harvests and uses as a key ingredient in the soups for which she is widely celebrated.

OPPOSITE

*Many elements of the garden are connected visually. Here, a profusion of ferns anchors the view across the long single-slab bridge toward the peony pavilion on the left and the house above to the right.*

LEFT & ABOVE

*An antique Japanese temple bell invites visitors to cross the bridge, which is just out of sight to the right of the bell post.*

OPPOSITE

*Our hellebores begin blooming in February and continue well into the summer. The moist soil in front of the rock face just across the bridge is ideal for both ferns and hellebores. Lichen in various hues of green proliferate on the rock outcroppings.*

LEFT

*The rustic stone bridge is repurposed from a salvaged twenty-foot-long piece of granite, once part of a large city building.*

OPPOSITE

*Son Palden Hamilton, a painter, captured the light on the forested hillside on the eastern slope of the stream valley.*

OPPOSITE

*Early spring narcissus in bloom along the stream.*

RIGHT

*To soften the transition into the forest, we naturalized azaleas, rhododendrons, and narcissus near the base of the hill, just to the east of the stream.*

OPPOSITE
*Ice begins to form on the surface of the stream after a cold winter's night.*

ABOVE
*The purple cones of a Norway spruce.*

RIGHT
*Bamboo casts a shadow on snow-covered ground on a late winter afternoon.*

LEFT

*Narcissus and trees frame the view of two bronze deer on a mound east of the stream. Note the trunk of a dead tree, called a snag, left standing to provide habitat for birds, insects, and other critters.*

OPPOSITE

*Spring color near the banks of the stream.*

FOLLOWING

*This Japanese Shinto shrine has been converted for Buddhist use. It contains a gilt bronze image of Sakyamuni, the historical Buddha. The final steps leading to the shrine are flanked with Chinese enameled bronze lanterns.*

OPPOSITE

*This natural stone outcropping comes into view as soon as one crosses the long bridge. We've positioned Japanese* jizo *statues, made in the image of the compassionate deity Jizo Bosatsu, and other figures as guardians for children and others who may pass.*

RIGHT

*A granite image of Japanese Buddhist deity Fudo Myo-o, spirit of enlightenment and slayer of illusions*

## The Japanese Gate, Hillside Sanctuary, and Stone Steps

SEVERAL HUNDRED YARDS NORTH of the stone bridge, the character of the stream changes: increasingly, large boulders define the stream edges and create small cascades as the stream rises in elevation. Large rocky outcroppings seem to grow out of the steep hillside, evidence of Maryland's last ice age more than 10,000 years ago. The lawns that lead down to the stream narrow and quickly disappear. It is this forested stream valley that most suggests the landscapes of Sikkim, and our treatment of this area reflects that sensibility.

Near the streamside we erected a Japanese bamboo gate that leads to a granite slab pathway. As the path winds its way through moss-covered boulders, the sound and sight of the flowing stream invite quiet contemplation. Granite pagodas, lanterns, and other figures installed among the boulders and on the nearby hillside reinforce the spiritual dimension that we and others experience in this part of the garden.

To connect this part of the property to the others, we planted numerous Japanese maples as understory trees. Each is enclosed by a bamboo fence, which adds a decorative element and protects the trees from bucks that would otherwise destroy them during the annual rut.

A dirt path leads farther into the forest to a granite post, which marks the beginning of one of our simplest-looking, yet most difficult, projects. To connect the valley to the trail system at the top of the hill, we installed a ten-story-high winding granite staircase. Set among huge boulders, each of the 120 individual steps weighs almost three hundred pounds. It took a crew of five, under the direction of stonemason Rob Stegman, three weeks of backbreaking work to manhandle and set each step. We like to think of this as our stairway to heaven.

OPPOSITE

*The Japanese gate marks the transition from open lawns to a more intimate section of the garden next to the stream.*

LEFT, OPPOSITE & FOLLOWING

*The stone paths between the Japanese gate and the stream are filled with texture and color in all seasons. The winding path encourages viewers to look down, pause, and reflect.*

LEFT

*The long trunks of poplar trees along the stream in summer.*

OPPOSITE

*Late afternoon light bathes the trees that grow on the hill on the east side of the stream valley. From a distance, they seem to glow as if on fire.*

PREVIOUS PAGES

*Stone monks, lanterns, pagodas, and moss-covered boulders form the hillside sanctuary. This area evokes a sense of spirituality and invites each viewer to quiet meditation.*

LEFT

*Hellebores and ferns grow from the forest floor, portending the arrival of spring.*

OPPOSITE

*Wild trout lilies compete with unfurling native Christmas ferns next to the forest path.*

OPPOSITE

*As the narcissus fade, Virginia bluebells take center stage amid the boulders. The Japanese granite lantern marks the beginning of the stone steps that lead to the ridge above.*

RIGHT

*A Virginia bluebell blooms in mid-spring.*

FOLLOWING LEFT

*Partially hidden by understory trees in spring, the stone steps captured in a drone view.*

FOLLOWING RIGHT

*A late autumn view looking down from halfway up the stone steps.*

CHAPTER SEVEN

# The Garden in Use

OPPOSITE
*One of the simple joys of childhood: looking for pebbles and minnows in the stream.*

FOLLOWING LEFT
*An art class paints a model at the peony pavilion.*

FOLLOWING RIGHT
*A local garden club explores the garden near the stream.*

WE WALK THROUGH our garden every day, Tsognie as part of her morning meditation, and I for the sheer pleasure and satisfaction that comes with being outside in nature. But for us, nothing is more rewarding than the sights and sounds of children running, swimming, stream exploring, lake kayaking, tree climbing, and koi feeding. We believe the best way to instill respect for the natural world in our granddaughters is to raise them in that very world.

We are always ready to welcome the many garden clubs that express interest in visiting, some from as far away as New York. There is a practical reason for our openness as well. Scheduling a tour provides a strong incentive to finish projects and attend to deferred maintenance. Plus, it is always a joy to compare notes with the numerous knowledgeable folks who visit, many of whom are more conversant about horticulture than we are.

## Bhutanese Archery Festival

The first thing Tsognie did after we acquired our property in 1998 was to put up Himalayan Buddhist prayer flags in order to bless the land. Within weeks, someone told us there were similar flags on a large farm about a mile and a half away. My first thought was that someone had hung out their laundry or installed flags for some other purpose. After all, what was the likelihood that two families in the same rural community in northern Baltimore County would share an affinity for the remote Himalayas? Shortly after, however, we met the owners and discovered that they enjoyed a multigenerational association with Bhutan and Bhutan's royal family, in the same way that my family had with Sikkim, Bhutan's immediate neighbor to the west. We naturally became friends.

One day, several years later, while Tsognie was in Sikkim, they invited me to lunch to meet a young Bhutanese man who was staying with them for the weekend. During the course of our conversation, he lamented that there was nowhere in America for the growing community of Bhutanese expats living in the U.S. to engage in archery, an activity that is both cultural and athletic. I believe I said, "I have a field." And so began our annual Bhutanese Archery Festival, which we have now held every Labor Day weekend for nearly two decades. Our neighbors join us in sponsoring the event. Each year, we invite hundreds of friends and friends of friends who might or do have an interest in Bhutan to join us throughout the competition.

PREVIOUS LEFT

*Bhutanese archers and their families. Seated in the front row in the pale blue blouse is the Honorable Doma Tshering, Ambassador and Permanent Representative of Bhutan to the United Nations.*

PREVIOUS RIGHT

*Near the conclusion of the archery competition, Bhutanese participants and their families invite other guests to join them in a traditional circle dance.*

CLOCKWISE FROM RIGHT

*The moment the archer releases his arrow; the best archer is carried off the range; each time an archer hits the target, at a distance of 145 meters, his teammates sing and perform a celebratory dance.*

OPPOSITE

*In the spirit of the competition, it is permissible for competitors' mates to try to distract and otherwise break the concentration of opposing archers as they prepare to shoot.*

OPPOSITE

*For many of the Bhutanese children, the pool is the highlight of the weekend.*

CLOCKWISE FROM LEFT

*Granddaughter Charlotte and friends enjoy the tube slide; our family group in Sikkimese attire; son Palden with his niece Charlotte and daughters Alice and Tara*

The actual tournament begins just before eight in the morning on Saturday with a prayer ceremony and continues through late Sunday afternoon. The competitors wear their national dress throughout the tournament, even in the heat and, at least once, through a heavy rain. Two or three teams of approximately a dozen archers compete to hit targets set 145 meters apart, a considerable distance. There is much good-natured taunting, especially among the women, who try to distract their mates' opponents while urging their partners to greater accuracy. At the end of each day's competition, we invite all to enjoy an elaborate buffet dinner served next to the house, with folks seated in tents, the pool pavilion, and the house, or settling down on the lawn, picnic style.

Hosting such an event takes a great deal of work and preparation. I am often asked why we do it—and the larger answer is we wish to support the celebration of traditional Himalayan culture in a fast-changing world. It also gives our sons and grandchildren, as well as the visiting Bhutanese young people, an occasion to wear their national dress while observing an event actively practiced in both Sikkim and Bhutan.

But there are other rewards. On the Friday afternoon of a recent tournament, I approached a small girl—perhaps seven years old—who was sitting by the pool waiting for the lifeguard to arrive. I welcomed her and asked how she was. She responded, "I was so excited to come here that I couldn't sleep last night." Then on Monday morning, while a crew of Bhutanese men joined me in disassembling part of the archery range, one of the archers approached me. "All the happiness to us, all the blessings to you," he said.

OPPOSITE
*The evening before the competition, a group of archers and their families gather around a fire to sing and dance, with much teasing between the men and women.*

RIGHT
*The competition ends on Sunday night with a fireworks display, here shown reflecting on the lake.*

# Land Preservation and Shared Use

In the early 1960s, a forward-thinking group of land planners created the Urban-Rural Demarcation Line (URDL) on a map of Baltimore County, with the goal of preserving the rural and farming character of a large portion of the county. Commercial and residential development was encouraged in specified areas closer to the city through higher-density zoning and the creation of infrastructure including roads and public sewer and water. Our property is included in the rural area protected by the URDL. In addition, since 1975 more than 68,000 acres in the county have been preserved through land preservation easements, ranking Baltimore County in the top ten counties in the nation for land preserved. Approximately two-thirds of our property is protected by preservation easements.

Almost three miles of walking/bridle trails wind through our forest. They connect with our neighbor's trails to form a large contiguous tract of land that is available to the local community for walking or riding. This includes providing access to the Green Spring Valley Hounds & Hunt Club, our local fox hunting club. Members are among the strongest local advocates for land preservation. Fox hunting is more of a chase than a hunt. The hounds are trained to follow the scent of a fox, who leads the hounds, followed by the field of riders, over open agricultural land, up and down steeply forested embankments, and across streams. The hunt is a cultural event with a rich history, not unlike Bhutanese archery. The fox, when it tires, goes to ground, often in an abandoned groundhog den where it is safe from the hounds. Only rarely is the fox caught, and then it is usually because it is diseased.

In this part of Baltimore County, landowners take stewardship of their property seriously, and many are generous in allowing community members to ride or walk through their properties. Western Run Valley is filled with committed land preservationists aware that their properties contribute to the Western Run–Belfast Road Historic District, with its rich rural character of farmland and historic homes.

ABOVE

*Neighbors are always welcome to ride through our property. We maintain approximately three miles of walking/bridle paths.*

OPPOSITE

*Members of the Green Spring Valley Hounds & Hunt Club gather with their hounds before the hunt.*

CHAPTER EIGHT

# Art & the Garden

AT THE TIME TSOGNIE AND I PURCHASED our first home—a modest row house in the inner suburbs of Baltimore—we were in our mid-twenties. In the small backyard of that house, we constructed a rock garden, our inaugural effort as emerging gardeners. At the same time, we began building our library and, consistent with our limited budget, purchasing several works of art.

OPPOSITE
*The warm oranges and reds of Japanese maple leaves contrast with the cool gray of granite.*

As Tsognie and I built our lives together, our interest in art and culture, nourished by extensive travel in both Europe and Asia, deepened. Just as books inform and tell stories, so do works of art. Interpreting and understanding those works, through research and observation, is one of the great joys of collecting. Drawing parallels between our garden and the themes reflected in the objects we collect has deepened our appreciation of both.

Our most focused collections include Japanese ceramics, painting, and lacquer. Several of these works are featured in this chapter. Many are on permanent display in our house.

Some of the pairings of garden photographs and art reflect simple visual similarities. In other combinations, the garden design represents visually the underlying philosophical tenets expressed in the accompanying work of art.

## Water Features

For thousands of years, water features have been an important element of gardens across the world, from ancient Mesopotamia to Rome, China, Japan, India, Persia, and other places. Water appeals to humans and animals alike; indeed, the wildlife that dwells in or about our lake and stream is paramount to our enjoyment of our property. We introduced Japanese koi to the lake early on, and feeding the eighty or so resident koi has become a regular ritual for us, our granddaughters, and our guests. We strike a rock against the teahouse deck and within thirty seconds the water is teeming with swirling color.

BELOW

*Two Japanese lacquer boxes capture the essence of water. The contemporary box on the left was made by Kyoto lacquer artist Zohiko the Tenth. The unsigned early-twentieth-century box on the right depicts fish and rock lobsters, reminding us of the crayfish that populate our stream.*

## Tree Peonies

Tree peonies are a favorite subject in both Japanese and Chinese art. Depending on the source, peonies are symbolic of ephemerality, bashfulness, beauty, wealth and abundance, good fortune, honor, spring, bravery, healing, and eternal and erotic love. These are heavy assignments, even for a flower with the beauty of a peony.

To Tsognie and me, they represent the fleeting nature of beauty and, perhaps, life itself. With extravagant blossoms and sublime scent, peonies are the most fragile of flowers. They are heavier than the stems on which they bloom, with the result that they fall over or break without additional support. Too much sun or heat, and they fade in a day or two. Rain breaks them apart whether they are partially or fully open. Regardless, they are stars in the arbors that adjoin our peony pavilion and remain one of our favorite flowers.

OPPOSITE LEFT

*A peony rendered in lacquer and inset mother-of-pearl decorates a large Japanese imperial presentation box. Produced in the first decade of the twentieth century, this work is identified as an imperial piece because of the sixteen-petaled chrysanthemum* mon, *or crest, used only by the emperor or his close family. The Tokugawa shoguns of the Edo period used a paulownia flower as their* mon. *In a society remarkable for its martial history, the use of flowers as important symbols is notable.*

OPPOSITE RIGHT

*An early twentieth-century vase depicting a tree peony blowing in the breeze.*

# Qianlong Bodhisattva

To say that a work of art speaks to us may seem trite, but it is nonetheless an apt explanation for why some objects appeal and others do not. Perhaps our attraction to a specific piece results from an association to something in our experience, or possibly to some aspect of our subconscious life. Why do some gardens give us a sense of belonging, whereas others lead us to feel we are mere observers?

A bodhisattva is a being who, despite approaching enlightenment, chooses out of compassion to stay and help guide other sentient beings in their quest to overcome their attachment to samsara—the cycle of birth, existence, and death—and the suffering that ensues. Because the attributes of the piece we acquired are missing (attributes are ritual objects held in the hands of religious figures), we are unable to identify which bodhisattva this is, but we know it is one of hundreds or perhaps thousands commissioned by the Qianlong emperor as a gift for his mother. It was made in the imperial workshops and bears Qianlong's mark. Qianlong's mother, Lady Niohuru, was a devout practitioner of Tibetan Buddhism, which is the root of Tsognie's faith.

OPPOSITE

*The prayer flags Tsognie maintains at Tashiding are for the benefit of all sentient beings. Block printed with prayers in Tibetan, the flags wave in the wind, distributing the blessings far and wide. In the Buddhist Himalayas, similar prayer flags stand at every monastery, shrine, hilltop, and mountain pass.*

RIGHT

*I was in my early twenties when I first saw this Chinese Qianlong-period (1735–1796) gilt bronze bodhisattva in the home of close older friends. I had a visceral attraction to it, not unlike the first time I saw the great pyramids at Giza, the Taj Mahal, or, indeed, Kanchenjunga at sunrise. Why should it be so? After my friends' deaths, their son, to whom I am also very close, generously allowed me to purchase this bronze from their estate. It resides in my study, facing my desk, where it epitomizes both compassion and extraordinary kindness.*

## Beauty in Small Things

Finding beauty in a garden often has little to do with our work as gardeners; rather, it involves how we see the little things that are around us all the time.

LEFT

*A contemporary Japanese incense box by Yamazaki Mushū, decorated in high-relief lacquer depicting five ants on beech leaves*

OPPOSITE

*We have paired the lacquer box on this page with photographs of a core and cross section of the ant-eaten stump of a dead apple tree.*

To see a World in a Grain of Sand
And a Heaven in a Wild Flower
Hold Infinity in the palm of your hand
And Eternity in an hour

—WILLIAM BLAKE

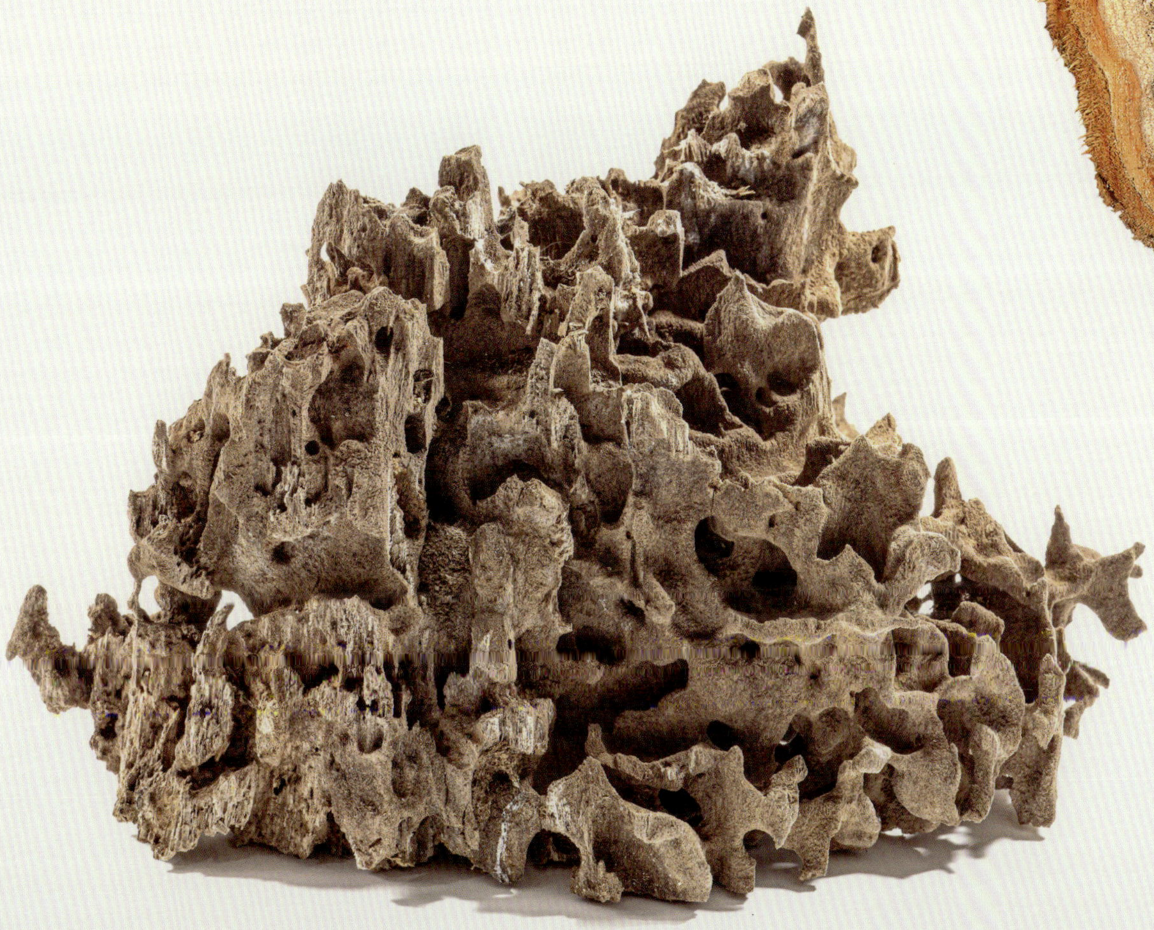

# Realms of the Dragon and Tiger

How to explain the unknowable? Every culture has its own mythology, based on what is known. How, then, to understand the energy and fecundity of the natural world? There are many variations on this theme, some of which overlap and some of which do not. I often sit on the veranda of the teahouse and watch thunderstorms approach from the west. Dark, swirling clouds and loud peals of thunder stir the blood. With the rain comes an intense scent of water, soil, and trees. The cool rain hitting the warmer water of the lake results in a soft fog that rises even as the rain falls with increased intensity.

I have experienced similar scenes many times in the mountains of Sikkim, Japan, and China. Lands of the thunderbolt. Realms of the dragon and tiger. According to Professor Marion Parris Smith, writing in a 1924 article for *Asia* magazine, "In *I Ching, The Book of Change*, attributed to the mythical First Emperor, Fu Hsi, and edited by Confucius, we find the cosmos described as controlled by two opposite, but harmonious, principles. The earth and terrestrial elements are ruled by the passive, female principle, Yin, the heavens and the celestial elements by the active, male principle, Yang. The tiger is the symbol of Yin; its nature is of earth, the solid substance. The dragon is the symbol of Yang; its nature is of water, clouds, and mist, the fluid substances. All created things result from the interaction of these opposite, but supplementary, principles."

OPPOSITE
*Boulders in the lake are a solid presence anchoring the reflected realm of sky and trees.*

LEFT
*In this exceptional mid-nineteenth-century Japanese Hirado porcelain* mizusashi, *or water jar, the artist depicts a terrestrial tiger on one side and a celestial dragon on the obverse.*

## Sun and Moon

The word *Dawa* means "moon" or "Monday" in Tibetan and is a popular name for both boys and girls in the Himalayan region. *Nyima* is Tibetan for "sun" or "Sunday," and is likewise a popular name for children of either gender. Full moon days are particularly significant for Tibetan, Sikkimese, and Bhutanese Buddhist practitioners, who believe that on those days all deeds and actions, good or bad, are considerably amplified. These days are marked by praying, performing *kora* (circumnavigations) of sacred sites, abstaining from eating meat, and performing acts of charity.

BELOW & OPPOSITE
*Early twentieth-century Japanese moon painting by Takeuchi Muyuju; the morning sun rising over the small island in the lake at Tashiding*

## Ono no Komachi

Ono no Komachi was a leading poet from tenth-century Japan. Most of her extant poems deal with lost love and erotic yearning. Though she was considered a great beauty in her youth, a popular portrayal of her in Japanese art depicts her as old, decrepit, and impoverished. She writes:

So lonely am I
My body is a floating weed
Severed at the roots.
Were there water to entice me,
I would follow it, I think.

—TRANSLATED BY DONALD KEENE

OPPOSITE, LEFT & RIGHT
*Autumn leaves in the streambed are framed by ice; view from the cut stone platform near the stream, looking past the decaying stump of a hundred-year-old tree toward the stream*

RIGHT
*A superb Meiji-era (1868–1912) wood and lacquer okimono, or ornament, depicting Ono no Komachi, who is shown seated on a log, perhaps contemplating both her past and her impending death.*

# Bamboo

Tsognie has introduced several species of bamboo that grow in our latitude, despite temperatures that occasionally drop to single digits. There are approximately thirty species of bamboo in Sikkim, growing from the tropical south through the temperate regions farther north. Bamboo, which is actually a perennial arborescent grass, is one of the most versatile plants in the world, providing food, construction material, paper pulp, and raw material for hundreds of other uses. At Tashiding, we use bamboo for fences, prayer flag poles, and screens. We especially value it for its elegant growth habit and foliage in all seasons.

RIGHT

*A Japanese ceramic studio vase depicting windswept bamboo leaves in relief, rendered in light blue and set against a cobalt blue background. This vase was made by Chuji Fukagawa, circa 1900.*

OPPOSITE

*The culms of nude sheath bamboo (*Phyllostachys nuda*) at Tashiding*

Be like bamboo.
The higher you grow,
the deeper you bow.

—CHINESE PROVERB

## Pines

A grove of pine trees grew at the edge of the hayfield at Emerald Hill, my childhood home. When I was in my early to mid-teens, I often climbed as high as I could in one of the taller trees. I have a vivid memory of one such day. Perched high in my special tree, which swayed rather violently to the vanguard wind of an approaching thunderstorm, I clung tightly to the rough bark, the wind in my face and the fragrance of pine tar in my nose. I recall feeling an intense longing to grasp the abstraction of my future life. That yearning stayed with me, leading years later to my solitary journey to the East, where so much of what was abstract took form.

At Tashiding, we have planted numerous examples of trees that are found in Sikkim. These include Deodar cedar, Himalayan pine, and Japanese cedar, first planted by the British in the Himalayas in the late nineteenth century and now widespread in the region.

No writing on the solitary, meditative dimensions of life can say anything that has not already been said better by the wind in the pine trees.

—THOMAS MERTON

OPPOSITE
*The bluish-green needles of a Himalayan pine (*Pinus wallichiana*), sometimes called a Bhutan pine, one of many we have planted at Tashiding.*

RIGHT
*A six-fold screen of an ancient Japanese black pine painted in 1915 by Japanese artist Imao Keinen.*

# Eight Immortals of the Wine Cup

This Hirado *mizusashi*, or water jar, was made to be used in the Japanese tea ceremony. It was created in the Japanese coastal city of Mikawachi by descendants of Korean potters who were brought to Japan in the seventeenth century to introduce the production of high-fired porcelain. This example was produced around 1800. The illustration depicted is based on a poem written in the eighth century by Chinese poet Du Fu, who is seated to the left on the jar. The theme of this work is the "eight immortals of the wine cup." This poem is a bit of a parody of the folk belief in the eight Taoist immortals, or sages. Du Fu and his fellow poets were all celebrated for their literature and excessive drinking. On this *mizusashi*, they are depicted in an idealized landscape inspired by traditional Chinese painting. Chinese themes like these were very popular in Japan because they recalled the ancient history of China from which Confucian thought, government, art, and literature originated, and which Japanese scholars considered the root of their own culture. The interpretation of the Hirado *mizusashi* is courtesy of my friend Dr. Robert Mintz, a noted Japanese scholar, curator, and museum administrator.

RIGHT
*Hirado* mizusashi, *or water jar*

OPPOSITE
*This photograph of the stream at Tashiding generates a sense of an idealized landscape, the stone walls giving a sense of age, while the flowering shrubs and trees suggest seasonal change and impermanence.*

PART THREE

# THE SIKKIM STORY

CHAPTER NINE

# The Royal Connection

PREVIOUS PAGE

*Son Douglas III sits between his grandfather, Sikkim Chogyal Palden Thondup Namgyal, and his great-grandmother, Kunzang Dechen, queen mother of Sikkim, at the annual ceremonial dances at the palace, winter 1980–81.*

OPPOSITE

*Buddhist Himalayan prayer flags at Tashiding*

After all these years, it is difficult to believe that, after arriving in New Delhi in 1972, I did not sleep for six full days and nights—but it is nonetheless true. Tsognie and I became inseparable. For a week, she cut her classes at Lady Shri Ram College, considered the finest women's college in India. Together we explored the city.

India was a cornucopia of sensory wonders: the odor of cow dung mixed with the sweet fragrance of jasmine, and copper-skinned women draped in saris of every color of the rainbow. Even the poorest-looking women seemed to adorn their ears, wrists, and ankles with gold jewelry. I wanted to see as much of the city as I could, to breathe in as much of it as possible. I still did not know where my life was headed, but I sensed that I had crossed a threshold and that the experience would alter the trajectory of my life.

Despite Tsognie's distress at the daily temperatures, which peaked above 110 degrees in the afternoon, she was a willing tour guide. We toured the Qutb Minar and Delhi's Red Fort; we walked endlessly through the city, including Connaught Place and the labyrinthine alleyways of Old Delhi, which teemed with people and shops filled with open sacks of colorful and aromatic spices. We scrambled over the ruins of the fort at Tughlakabad, the fourteenth-century mausoleum of the first ruler of the Tughlaq dynasty, and took long walks in Lodi Gardens at dusk. The reality was that Tsognie and I were both strangers in a strange land. Sikkim is a couple of thousand miles from New Delhi, and a world away in terms of culture, language, and ethnicity. I am certain many of the places we visited together were new to her as well, but after several years in Delhi, Tsognie had learned the language and knew how to navigate the city.

I still knew little of Tsognie's background or her connection to the palace in Sikkim. She seemed to enjoy being somewhat mysterious. We were lost in our own bubble. As the days went on, I became more curious and perhaps a bit apprehensive. Everything about her manner and poise suggested she was highborn. I began to worry that our liaison might be breaking some taboo that would lead to difficult consequences. I was in Asia, after all, and had little familiarity with social norms and constructs.

Courtesy of my family connection, I had an invitation to visit Sikkim that autumn as a palace guest. My first introduction to Sikkim had occurred more than ten years earlier, when I was eleven years old. My Aunt Elaine, my father's younger sister, had invited the then-widowed crown prince of Sikkim and his young American fiancée, Hope Cooke, to spend a week at Emerald Hill. The prince and Hope were on a tour of the States. My aunt, as his close friend, thought a week in the country might prove a welcome respite in the midst of their busy schedule. Throughout the 1960s, all the major American magazines ran stories about the "prince of Shangri-la" and his American bride, and there was much hoopla surrounding the couple's visit. My cousins and sisters and I were to be on our best behavior, which we were, at least until my two-year-old sister sat on the prince's head as he lay by the pool. He found this quite amusing, though in his world this sort of behavior was most definitely not something to be condoned.

One evening, about a week after Tsognie and I met, I urged her to tell me about her family. Though a bit reluctant, she in time told me her father was, in fact, the Chogyal, or king, of Sikkim. At the time she was conceived, she said, her mother and her father, then the crown prince, were in a serious love affair when his parents decided it was time for him to marry. For Sikkimese princes, this meant only one thing: an arranged marriage to a woman from one of the aristocratic families of Tibet. The royal

OPPOSITE
*Tsognie at Emerald Hill, my family home in Maryland, in October 1973, shortly before our engagement.*

LEFT
*The "asking ceremony" at the palace, in which I formally asked Zhungkiang for his permission to marry his daughter; from left: my aunt Elaine Hamilton; me, the expectant groom; Tsognie's mother, Kaden (our first meeting); and Zhungkiang, April 1974.*

FOLLOWING
*Tsognie and her mother, May 1974, after our wedding.*

family of Sikkim were Bhutias, from Tibetan stock: Tsognie's mother was Lepcha, the indigenous people who lived in Sikkim before the ascendancy of the first Bhutia king some three hundred years ago. A marriage between them was not possible.

I will fast-forward this narrative to an evening at the palace in Sikkim twenty-one months later. Tsognie and I had been married several days earlier in an elaborate ceremony. After dinner, the Chogyal, or Zhungkiang (a slightly less formal title for His Highness, which I will use henceforth), invited me to join him in the library of the palace. On a table in the corner, surrounded by shelves of books, were two glasses and two bottles of Châteauneuf-du-Pape.

He invited me to sit in one of the two armchairs present, poured each of us a glass of wine, and began to talk. He spoke of his life and the challenges he faced as he struggled to maintain Sikkim's sovereignty as a small country sandwiched between Chinese Tibet to the north and India to the south. He asked me more about my family and my plans. We drank and talked all night. The bottles were empty when the sky began to lighten. He leaned forward to make certain he had my full attention, then spoke plainly. He described the love he had shared with Tsognie's mother, that it had not been possible for them to marry, and that Ongmu (his affectionate name for Tsognie) was conceived intentionally as a lasting testament to their love. He described what a wonderful woman

Tsognie's mother, Kaden, was, that her daughter's marriage and move to the States would be difficult for her, and that I should always treat Kaden with kindness and respect. He went on to extol Tsognie's intelligence and athletic abilities, then gently warned me that she could, at times, be "very stubborn and willful." He finished with this admonishment: "Ongmu is a wonderful girl, and I expect real consideration." His sadness at her moving so far away was palpable.

But all this was in the future as I sat talking with Tsognie in the Sikkim guesthouse in New Delhi, trying to process the challenge we faced. Tsognie needed to get back to college, and it was time for me to begin my exploration of India before heading northeast to the Himalayas. Within days, Tsognie returned to her hostel (similar to a dorm) at Lady Shri Ram and I headed by train to Agra and Fatehpur Sikri, then flew south to visit the erotic temples at Khajuraho. I decided to stop in Delhi again for a few days before flying to Bagdogra Airport near Siliguri in West Bengal, which was the gateway to Darjeeling and the monastery where I intended to study.

That visit to Delhi proved more complicated than I had hoped. Now that Tsognie was back in the hostel it was difficult for her to get out without a good reason. Tsognie's cousin and my friend, Princess Sodeun-la, had returned from Hong Kong and was able to "free" Tsognie for a short weekend, but now we all shared Sodeun-la's small quarters in the guesthouse. As soon as Tsognie returned to college, I departed for the Himalayas. We promised to write to each other. And write we did. I would send letters to her at the hostel and she to me care of the Windamere Hotel in Darjeeling, which would become my address when I was not at the monastery. Our romance, which began with such passion, grew and deepened through our exchange of letters.

We both understood the necessity of keeping our association confidential. Tsognie was of marriageable age; any hint of a romance with an American might well have resulted in pressure for her to marry a more suitable Sikkimese. And there were suitors already making overtures.

Several months later, I returned to Delhi with deepened insight into Tsognie's culture. I understood more fully the challenges we faced but seeing her again only steeled my resolve. I was out of money and needed to return to the States to begin my career. Tsognie needed to finish her education and return to Sikkim to help support her father as India's political noose on Sikkim tightened. The odds against us seemed insurmountable. Tsognie made a vague promise to try to visit the U.S. the following year. We said our goodbyes at Sikkim House before I left for the airport. I did not know whether or how I would ever see her again.

I arrived back in the U.S. weeks later, in November of 1972, after having spent time with my Aunt Elaine at her home near Paris. I returned to a small batch of letters from Tsognie, and thus began the next chapter of our story. We wrote to each other almost daily, numbering each letter on the envelope so we would not read them out of order. The post both ways in those days was erratic; a letter might take a week or two or three to arrive. Calling on the phone was out of the question. Not only were the phone lines undependable, booking a call was also prohibitively expensive.

Autumn turned to winter, then the snows of winter melted away to signs of spring. We continued to write. In May, Tsognie graduated from college and returned to Sikkim, where political tensions were increasing by the week. As spring turned to summer, it became clear that Zhungkiang's marriage to Hope was nearing its final chapter. By late summer, Hope left for New York City for good, bringing her two children and Yangchen, Zhungkiang's daughter and youngest child with Sangay Deki, his deceased Tibetan wife. His two older sons, including Crown Prince Tenzing, remained in Britain, where they continued their studies. Money was tight: getting foreign exchange to settle his youngest children in New York required government approval, giving Indian officials an opportunity to make his personal life more difficult even as they sought to undermine his government. (With the lapse of British paramountcy in India in 1947, Sikkim had negotiated a treaty with independent India. By mutual agreement, the so-called 1950 treaty made Sikkim a protectorate of newly independent India. Under the agreement, Sikkim retained full responsibility for its domestic affairs, whereas India assumed responsibility for Sikkim's communications, defense, foreign policy, and currency.)

## Overcoming Obstacles

It was against this complicated backdrop that I expected Tsognie to ask if she could visit me in the States. In hindsight, I should have realized that this was not likely to happen. However deep her love for me, Tsognie's loyalty to her father was paramount. Our letters occasionally became a bit strained as this became more apparent. The possibility of me visiting Sikkim was equally difficult, as getting to Sikkim required palace assistance to gain the required permits. Even had I managed to arrive in Sikkim, I knew Tsognie would steer clear of me to avoid creating a scandal.

So, I asked my parents for assistance. For the better part of a year, they had observed the constant flow of letters back and forth. Photos of Tsognie were displayed on the night table next to my bed. My cousin Lee and her mother, Aunt Sparky, who lived in the other large house at Emerald Hill, actually met Tsognie before I had and developed a special affection for her. They had been in France staying with Aunt Elaine early in the summer of 1972 when Tsognie arrived for a two-week stay. Lee later told me they had found the perfect girl for me, though at the time, the chance of our meeting seemed remote. My parents wrote to Zhungkiang, asking if Tsognie could visit as their guest. Given the family connection, I thought this had a reasonable chance of success. Everyone at Emerald Hill knew there was a serious romance between us.

Zhungkiang's response to my parents' invitation was a polite no. Tsognie was aware of the invitation but, fearing the consequences of revealing the full reason for the invitation, accepted her father's decision without protest.

Pursuing an impossible romance and gardening on the scale of Tashiding require many of the same traits—perseverance, good luck, and a certain boldness. Sometimes in life one must create one's own luck, so I decided boldness was the order of the day. I wrote directly to Zhungkiang, telling him politely but clearly that there was a romance going on, that marriage had been discussed between us, and asking respectfully if he would allow Tsognie to visit. As it happened, on the day my letter arrived, he did not read his personal mail until midnight. Tsognie was summoned from bed to his presence; there were confessions, tears, and upset all around. Calls were made to my aunt in Paris; she, in turn, called me demanding an explanation. Days later, after hearing directly of Tsognie's resolve, Zhungkiang agreed to let her come. Within a week or two, Aunt Elaine flew to India, and then on to Sikkim to confer. She suggested that Tsognie travel with her to France before coming on to the States. I knew my aunt was angry with me, believing I was too young to marry, so I was not enthused by yet another delay, but Tsognie saw it as an act of affection, which was mostly true. The plan was set, and at the end of September 1973, after the requisite two weeks in France, Tsognie arrived at Emerald Hill for a two-month visit.

Tsognie's stay at Emerald Hill was a resounding success. Our extended separation and correspondence had allowed us to get to know each other without being blinded

by the passion that often masks incompatibility. Tsognie was lovingly embraced by every member of my extended family. Emerald Hill included two large family houses plus my grandmother's stone cottage, and three generations of the family moved freely in and out of one another's houses. Being outdoors was central to life at Emerald Hill; Tsognie and I spent days exploring the property's pastures, forest, and fields. She felt instantly at home.

Although my letter to Zhungkiang had served as the catalyst for our reunion, I understood that I had stepped outside the bounds of proper protocol with Tsognie's family. So, at this point, I decided the best course of action would be for Tsognie to return to Sikkim, with me to follow in four months or so to ask properly for her hand in marriage. Then, assuming success, we could marry the following year.

Tsognie left at the end of November to spend several days in New York with her half siblings and Hope, who had settled in an apartment on the Upper East Side of Manhattan. Tsognie planned to fly back to Sikkim immediately after her visit. Within a day of Tsognie's departure, my father asked what my intentions were. I explained my plan, to which he responded with the best and wisest counsel I have ever received in my life. "I wouldn't wait," he said. No doubt, he had conferred with my mother, who in Tsognie had discovered, as I had, a kindred spirit. But more than that, he understood intuitively that much is lost between the lip and the cup.

I called Tsognie in New York and told her I wanted to see her one more time before she departed. Hope graciously said I was free to stay with her and the children. Several days later, after purchasing a very simple and inexpensive ruby engagement ring (I still had little money), I took the train to New York. Upon arrival, I immediately asked Tsognie to take a walk with me along the East River, which was only a block or two away. Eventually, we found a park bench in front of Gracie Mansion, the mayor's official residence. I invited Tsognie to sit, got down on one knee, presented her with the ring, and asked her to marry me. At first, she looked bewildered. Men do not get down on one knee in Sikkim, nor are engagement rings part of their tradition. I had clearly confused her. It took a minute or so for her to comprehend fully what I was asking. But when she did, she answered, "I will, if my father approves."

In some respects, I felt that we were back where we started. But when we returned to the apartment, Hope was there to congratulate us. She was still the Gyalmo, or queen, of Sikkim and could not have been nicer. Although I had spent some time with

OPPOSITE TOP

*Tsognie, baby Douglas III, and Zhungkiang at our first home in Maryland, summer 1978.*

OPPOSITE BOTTOM

*Tsognie encourages Zhungkiang in a game of mahjong, late 1970s.*

ABOVE

*Members of the extended Sikkim royal family, including Douglas III (in front of his grandfather) and Tsognie and baby Palden on the right, winter 1980–81.*

FOLLOWING LEFT

*The wedding group, from left: Zhungkiang; me; Tsognie's mother, Kaden; Tsognie; Elaine Hamilton; and Lingtsang Gyalpo, the exiled Tibetan king of Ling.*

FOLLOWING RIGHT

*At a reception for government officials at the Nor-Khill Hotel in Gangtok, Tsognie and I cut the wedding cake. We enjoyed different receptions on three successive evenings.*

her in Sikkim on my first visit, this was an opportunity for us to become much better acquainted. My Aunt Elaine and Hope had for years suffered a rather antagonistic relationship, but it was clear that this would not color our interaction. Because space was at a premium in the apartment, bedding was prepared and Tsognie and I were more than content to sleep on the living room floor for the next several nights. Our happy interlude in New York was followed by yet another separation.

As soon as I returned to Baltimore, I got down to the serious business of writing to Zhungkiang again, this time to ask for Tsognie's hand in marriage. I extolled my virtues, as I saw them, declared my devotion and love for Tsognie, and related my family's approval and my prospects for supporting her. I anxiously awaited his reply. His response, which arrived two weeks later, was direct. "I'll come to the United States next month and we'll talk about it." Which he did.

Zhungkiang arrived in New York a month later. There were several reasons for his trip. I think he sought a reconciliation with Hope, which did not occur, and he missed his younger children. It must have seemed as though his world was collapsing on top of him, and, in reality, it was. Kings are not immune to suffering.

But he seemed in good spirits when he traveled to Baltimore to meet with me and my parents. Hope had apparently put in a good word for me. I believe that, in a way, he appreciated my perseverance and perhaps my boldness. In Himalayan cultures at that time, marriages were not merely the purview of the couple who might wish to marry. It was understood that romantic love was not the main consideration, though love often follows. For Zhungkiang's first marriage, his parents had selected his mate. Before meeting me, Tsognie had expected that her parents would "suggest" acceptable mates. She might have exercised her veto for candidates who were unappealing to her but would likely have accepted a young man suggested by, or certainly approved by, her parents. Once it became apparent that Tsognie and I had my parents' strong support, Zhungkiang gave his consent.

## The Wedding and Beyond

A Buddhist marriage ceremony was scheduled for late April 1974 in Sikkim, to be followed by a Christian ceremony in Baltimore in June. In the meantime, Tsognie and I were back to writing letters.

I arrived in Gangtok on April 23, two days before the wedding. Zhungkiang charged Tsognie's eldest uncle, acting on my behalf, with making certain all the required traditions were observed, which was good because I was completely oblivious to local custom. Among the most important of these was the "asking ceremony," which normally would have taken place well in advance of the wedding but was now scheduled for the morning of April 24. I saw Tsognie briefly the evening before. She explained that her father insisted that every aspect of the asking ceremony be carried out to perfection.

I arrived in the sitting room of the palace in the morning. Zhungkiang and Tsognie's mother, Kaden, whom I had never met, awaited my arrival. After respectfully performing my three requisite prostrations to Zhungkiang, I presented him with a ceremonial silk *kata*, or scarf. Shortly afterward, a delegation entered the room with "my" gifts to my prospective father-in-law. These included a sack of rice, a large basket of fermented millet used to make *chung*, the local beer, and half a dressed steer and pig. I felt as though I had stepped back in time to the court of Genghis Khan. But, perhaps oddly, I felt increasingly at home.

Every ceremony in Sikkim involves the active participation of the monastic community. Prayers commence days in advance of marriages, deaths, anniversaries of deaths, journeys, religious holidays, and the like. The roots of Buddhism, laced with an element of unique Sikkimese animistic practice, run deeply through every aspect of life. Zhungkiang selected two aged and highly accomplished *gomchens*, or "great meditators," to officiate at our wedding. Prayers by the attending monks continued throughout the wedding ceremony, which lasted late into the afternoon. Offerings were made on our behalf to the guardian spirits of the land, from all four directions, asking them to witness and bless our union, to accept and adopt me into the fold, and to provide their protection. Hundreds of guests joined the celebration. As each arrived, they entered the *lhakhang*, or shrine room (in our case in Tsognie's mother's house), to present us with *katas,* envelopes of cash, and other gifts.

The highlight was the arrival of Zhungkiang toward the end of the day. He entered with a flourish, unfurled two unusually large and precious silk katas, presented one to each of us, then reached inside the top of his *gho,* Sikkim's national dress. He produced a small gilt bronze figure of Sakyamuni, the historical Buddha, also wrapped in silk. This he presented to Tsognie with the admonition to never forget her homeland and to always practice her faith.

After the various receptions concluded, Tsognie and I headed north by jeep for a ten-day honeymoon, which was to include a week's trek in the remote mountains of northwest Sikkim, not far from the Tibetan border. We traveled with a palace cook, his assistant, and a box of goodies, which included a canned Danish ham, English biscuits, and several bottles of French cognac and champagne. In Lachen, the last village in north central Sikkim that could be reached by vehicle, we hired as porters five Lachen-pas, rugged but jolly men, to guide us through the mountains and carry most of our food and gear.

It was both Tsognie's and my first exposure to serious Himalayan trekking. Over the next glorious but challenging days we trekked through forests of rhododendrons, crossed two high, snow-covered passes, forged raging streams, and navigated dangerous slide areas. In doing so, we entered what some call the "throne room of the mountain gods," and were forever changed.

The challenges that Sikkim faced as an independent kingdom came into sharp focus after we returned to Gangtok. In honor of our marriage, Katyayani Shankar Bajpai, the Indian political officer (equivalent of ambassador), invited us and other dignitaries to a reception at his official residence, India House. Bajpai seemed a very high-level diplomat to be stationed in what was, on the surface, a minor posting. He later served as ambassador to Pakistan, China, and the United States, among the most important appointments for an Indian diplomat.

We prepared to leave the palace for India House shortly after dark. Normally, security at the palace was a rather low-key affair. Armed guards were always posted at the ceremonial gate located at the base of the palace ridge, but people seemed to come and go at will, often on their way to Tsuklakhang, the royal monastery. On this evening, however, everything seemed different, and slightly ominous. Tsognie and I walked out of the palace residence to find Zhungkiang's white Mercedes waiting between two jeeps filled with Sikkim guards, all armed to the teeth. As Tsognie, Zhungkiang, and I climbed into the back seat, with Tsognie in the middle, I noticed an additional armed guard seated in the front passenger seat. None of the guards were smiling.

As we drove across the palace ridge toward our destination, Zhungkiang reviewed with us who he expected to be there, individuals we should be sure to acknowledge and cultivate. He described the reception room where the event was to occur, then advised me to look for a door toward the back of the room. "Behind that door," he said, "they are plotting the takeover of my kingdom." We rode the rest of the way in silence. At the time, I did not realize the extent of the stress he was under, or the complex campaign of subversion the government of India and her minions had loosed upon him and his mission to preserve Sikkim's autonomy.

Tsognie and I left Sikkim for the States several days later, accompanied by Tsognie's mother and Kunga Nima, one of her younger uncles, who decades later became one of the most prominent and well-loved political leaders of the state. Sending family members to see a bride to her new home was a Sikkimese tradition, but I think the main reason was that Zhungkiang wanted to ease Kaden's concern over her daughter moving halfway around the world. They stayed with us for six weeks in the apartment near Emerald Hill I had rented a month before I left for Sikkim.

## The Last Chogyal of Independent Sikkim

Within a month of our return to the States, the political situation in Sikkim went from bad to worse. The best account of this period in Sikkim was written several years later by a prominent (and brave) Bengali journalist, Sunanda Datta-Ray. His book, *Smash and Grab: Annexation of Sikkim*, offers an accurate description of India's duplicity.

Though Tsognie missed her family, and despite the turmoil in Sikkim, we settled easily into married life. Tsognie had begun her boarding school education at age six and was thus used to long separations from home. She was not, however, used to reports of the sort we heard less than a year later as we watched the evening news on television. "According to reports coming out of the central Himalayan Kingdom of Sikkim," the reporter announced, "Indian troops have attacked the palace. The fate of the Chogyal, or king, is unknown."

Zhungkiang once described to me the first time he saw an Indian truck driver on the roads of Sikkim in the late 1940s or early 1950s. He told me he remembered thinking, "This is the thin edge of the wedge." Zhungkiang survived the attack, though the two guards at the gate had been shot, one mortally. Indian troops swept through Gangtok, beating and detaining anyone who might resist their takeover. The thick end of the wedge now dominated life in Sikkim.

India positioned troops around the entire palace complex, and for the next three years Zhungkiang was held, isolated and largely incommunicado. He had miscalculated India's resolve to swallow Sikkim, believing that many of the difficulties he had faced in recent years were the responsibility of "lower downs" in India's bureaucracy. He now realized that this final step, and the complete absorption of Sikkim that followed, could not have occurred without the express consent of Indira Gandhi, India's prime minister. His appeals to her fell on deaf ears.

India's takeover of Sikkim occurred in April 1975, the same month that the U.S. Embassy in Saigon was dramatically evacuated ahead of the North Vietnamese advance. World attention was focused elsewhere in Asia as India, billed as the world's largest democracy, absorbed tiny Sikkim, a nominal monarchy. In late June, just two months after attacking Sikkim, Indira Gandhi engineered a so-called national "emergency" within India and assumed dictatorial powers. More than 100,000 Indian citizens were arrested and detained. Before Prime Minister Gandhi eliminated freedom of the press, one Indian magazine carried an obituary that read, "Democracy, beloved husband of Truth, loving Father of Faith, Hope, and Justice, expired on June 26."

In November 1975, Tsognie returned to Sikkim for the first time since our marriage, and I followed a month later. I needed Indian government permission to enter and was given only a ten-day permit. The palace, which had been a center of Sikkim's cultural and political life, was deserted and sad. During that stay, and the others that followed in ensuing years, my admiration for Zhungkiang only increased. Though he never reconciled himself to Sikkim's loss of identity, the decline of his own status did not seem to concern him.

Tsognie and I returned less than a year later, again with her arriving a month ahead of me and my ten-day permit. India had incorporated the Sikkimese civil service personnel into the Indian civil service and flooded the country with money. Senior members of Sikkim's government who were suspected of loyalty to the palace had been relieved of their duties. Large numbers of residents of India and the neighboring Himalayan foothills began to move into Sikkim, overwhelming and diluting the indigenous population.

As we left Sikkim after our visit, an incident occurred that reminded us of the danger that existed in India under Indira Gandhi's "emergency," which continued. We traveled by jeep from Sikkim to Bagdogra Airport. From there, we flew to Delhi to catch our Pan American flight back to the States. Before boarding the plane in Delhi, we had to pass through armed Indian security, along with all other passengers. Tsognie carried an Indian "protected person" passport that listed her address as the palace in Sikkim. The Indian army captain in charge of security looked at Tsognie's credentials and refused to release her to board the plane. He obviously intended to detain her. I argued as best as I could, aware that he was armed and supported by several other armed soldiers. He refused to budge.

Reluctantly, I left Tsognie standing there and went in search of the Pan Am station manager. I found the Pan Am offices, pushed my way past several staff members, and entered the office of the manager, an Indian national. I explained the situation and sensed immediately that I had found the right person. We hurried through the airport back to the security check post, where Tsognie stood waiting. The Indian captain was clearly not pleased to see us. The Pan Am manager questioned the captain in alternating Hindi and English; their discussion quickly devolved into an open argument. The captain, faced with the assertiveness of such a senior person, instructed one of his assistants to place a call to the Home Office seeking guidance. All other passengers had boarded the plane, and I noted we were now past the scheduled departure time.

The standoff continued—the assistant could not get through on the telephone, and the captain looked increasingly agitated. Finally, the Pan Am manager looked him in the eye, and said, "These two passengers have tickets on this Pan American flight. And this flight is not going to depart without them, and you do not have the authority to hold up an international flight." The captain took one last look toward his subordinate, who continued trying, unsuccessfully, to book his call. Then, with an almost imperceptible quick nod of his head, he signaled that we could depart. The Pan Am manager immediately grabbed my hand on one side and Tsognie's on the other, led us down to the tarmac, found a car, and drove us out to the waiting jet. The door of the plane opened, the stairs were rolled up to the door, and with the urging of our rescuer, we climbed quickly up and into the airplane. Until Pan American ceased operations fifteen years later, I refused to travel on any other international air carrier.

The next eighteen months brought great happiness, then great tragedy. Our first son, Douglas III, was born in June 1977. In March 1978, the charismatic Crown Prince Tenzing was killed in an automobile accident just below the palace ridge in Sikkim. He died in his father's arms; any hope that the next generation of the royal family would provide a level of leadership died with him. In an ironic twist of fate, it had been Prince Tenzing who walked down to Kaden's house to inform her of the telegram we sent announcing Douglas III's birth. Zhungkiang visited us in the States that summer, and our young family traveled to Sikkim over the Christmas holidays later that year.

With the birth of our second son, Palden, in January 1980, we were unable to travel to Sikkim until December of that year, though Zhungkiang joined Kaden in Baltimore that summer to meet his namesake and second grandson.

By the end of 1980 and early 1981, India felt secure enough in its position to loosen the restrictions on Zhungkiang and what was left of the palace establishment. The important Kagye Cham rituals were held at Tsuklakhang, the royal chapel. The prayers and ritual dances conducted for this event are among the most important esoteric tantric practices of the Nyingma or "Red Hat" order of Tibetan Buddhism practiced by most Sikkimese.

While many Kagye Cham prayers and rituals involve the philosophical and secret teachings practiced and understood only by highly accomplished monks, there are elements designed to be accessible to a broader audience. These include visualizations of what a consciousness experiences after death and before rebirth, the so-called state of *bardo*. What one's consciousness sees, and how it reacts, is believed to determine the circumstances of one's rebirth.

Our son Douglas was then a mature three-and-a-half years old and Palden not quite one. Some of the pall that had descended on the palace lifted a bit, at least on the surface. Zhungkiang enjoyed the activity and commotion that resulted from having his two grandsons in the palace. He seemed especially fond of having Douglas near him, insisting he sit next to him in the royal tent overlooking the dances. We did not know then that this would be Zhungkiang's last Kagye Cham, or that he would be diagnosed less than a year later with cancer of the larynx, which led to surgery at Sloan Kettering in New York, followed by complications and his death on January 30, 1982. He was fifty-eight years old, fifty-nine by the Sikkimese calendar.

Kaden was visiting with us in Baltimore during Zhungkiang's surgery and convalescence. Thankfully, but sadly, she had the opportunity to say her final goodbye to him as he lay near death. She left for Sikkim immediately thereafter. Tsognie and I, with two small children at home in Baltimore, had only a day or two to prepare before departing for the funeral in Sikkim. Leaving Douglas and Palden with my parents, we flew first to New Delhi. Tsognie's half siblings and Zhungkiang's body had arrived at Sikkim House shortly before we did. Within hours, we departed for the Delhi airport, where the Indian government, in a rare gesture of goodwill, provided a military transport airplane for the flight to Bagdogra Airport at the base of the Himalayan foothills, the penultimate stop

on Zhungkiang's final return to his lost kingdom. We sat on the canvas seats that lined each side of the spare military aircraft. Zhungkiang's body, seated upright in the lotus position inside a simple wooden box, sat in front of us, draped in the red, yellow, and white colors of the Sikkim flag.

Zhungkiang's body rested in state at Tsuklakhang for close to three weeks, surrounded by an honor guard and rows of chanting monks. It rained all day, every day. We spent most of our time sitting silently in the chapel, reflecting on his death and the difficult last years of his life. A special group of monks were charged with conducting prayers to stop the rain on the day of the cremation. On the morning of the cremation, their efforts proved successful. The day dawned bright and clear. I and many others of his extended family joined in carrying the palanquin that held his remains out of the chapel and on three circumnavigations of the building before proceeding to the royal cremation grounds at Lukshama, several miles away. Thousands of Sikkimese lined the roads to observe and follow the procession. Later that afternoon, as the cremation ceremony neared its conclusion, the sky lowered and the rain resumed. It continued to rain through our departure for the States several days later.

OPPOSITE

*Zhungkiang's body rests in state, surrounded by an honor guard. Monks in the foreground perform the appropriate prayers, a process that continued daily for three weeks.*

RIGHT

*Zhungkiang's casket being carried to the cremation grounds, several miles away.*

FOLLOWING

*Kaden, in her nun's robes, and Tsognie.*

As soon as the funeral rituals concluded, Kaden left her home to spend most of the next year in a meditation hut on the Taktse ridge north of Gangtok. From Taktse, she had a clear view of the cremation grounds at Lukshama. Contemplating that even a king was inevitably reduced to a handful of ash, she made the decision to renounce the secular world and become a Buddhist nun. She took her vows in Bodh Gaya in India, where the Dalai Lama cut the final tuft of hair from her shaven head. She then spent three years and three months in seclusion and meditation, under the guidance and instruction of Dodrupchen Rinpoche, one of the preeminent clerics of the Nyingma Buddhist tradition. Kaden continues to spend part of each year with us in Baltimore. Every morning—rain, snow, or shine—she walks down to the Japanese teahouse on the lake to do her morning prayers, which last for several hours.

Sikkim today bears little resemblance to the rather simple and isolated mountain kingdom I first visited. Following the merger with India, tens of thousands of Indians settled in Sikkim, overwhelming the native population. Hamlets have become villages and small villages large towns. Gangtok now seems one continuous megalopolis of ugly concrete buildings. Walking paths to remote places have become roads, now accessible to

the throngs of Indians and tourists who visit Sikkim each year in search of mountain air and views.

Perhaps the most fitting epitaph for Zhungkiang came shortly after his death with a statement from the Sikkim Assembly, many members of which had been complicit in the Indian takeover several years earlier.

> During the hour of his trial, when his very throne was at stake, Chogyal Palden Thondup Namgyal stood like a rock and sacrificed petty considerations for the lofty ideals he had espoused. He lost, but in the very process of losing his throne and status, he rose to his full stature. For when "little men" who rule the roost in Sikkim will have been consigned to dust, posterity will look back with awe and respect upon the last representative of the House of Namgyal on the throne of Sikkim and say that Palden Thondup Namgyal bowed out of the political stage of Sikkim with the grace of a ruler and with the courage of a real man. He lost his Kingdom, but gained a martyr's halo. And his descendants will be able to walk with their heads held high whatever their circumstances in life happen to be.

Nearly fifty years after Sikkim lost its independence, and more than four decades after Zhungkiang's death, the Sikkim flag still flies every day in one place in the world. And that place is Tashiding, our garden in the Maryland countryside.

# POSTSCRIPT

OPPOSITE LEFT
*Tsognie and sons with Tsognie's paternal grandmother, Gyalum (queen mother) Kunzang Dechen.*

OPPOSITE RIGHT
*Tsognie and sons with her maternal grandmother, Pemkit Lepcha (center) and mother, Kaden.*

IN JANUARY 1981, THE DAY AFTER I was able to gather members of the extended royal family for a group photo, I organized members of Tsognie's maternal family on the palace lawn for a second photograph. The Shipputso clan are from the Lepcha ethnic group, Sikkim's original indigenous people before the Bhutias (of Tibetan stock) migrated from the north in the seventeenth century, followed by an influx of Nepalese from the south beginning in the nineteenth century. The Bhutias, from whom the royal family are descended, quickly established themselves as the small nation's aristocracy. The industrious Nepalese settled the southern and western portions of Sikkim, eventually becoming the majority population.

The Lepchas call themselves Motangchi Rongkup, or Rong for short, which translates as "children of nature." Buddhism as it exists in Sikkim today owes much to the animistic practice of the original Lepcha people. As the influence of the royal family diminished after the absorption of Sikkim into India and the deaths of Crown Prince Tenzing in 1978 and

Zhungkiang in 1982, Tsognie's maternal family established itself as one of the most successful and influential in Sikkim.

Tsognie's grandmother, Pemkit, and grandfather, Chungu Shipputso, had nine children who survived to adulthood. Their eldest daughter, Kaden, bore Zhungkiang two children: Tsognie and a younger son, Nawong Jigme, who sadly died of illness in 1957, just after his fifth birthday. Since taking her vows as a Buddhist nun in 1984, Amla (Sikkimese for "mother") has pursued her religious practice and, at age ninety-three, still serves as the head nun at Tsengen Ugen Chocorling nunnery. With Tsognie's support, the nunnery has just completed a total renovation and expansion.

The practice of Buddhism forms the cultural and ethical foundation for the entire family. Kaden's brother, Lama Samdrub Lepcha, a highly respected religious teacher, began his career as an itinerant monk, traveling through Tibet, Bhutan, and Ladakh, where he received teachings from many of the most revered Buddhist masters of his day. Back in Sikkim, he became an important part of the leadership of Enchey Monastery, where he established a school for young monks.

As a Nyingma sect monk, Samdrub eschewed vows of chastity and married, producing six children, including son Tulku Pema. As a boy, Tulku was recognized as the reincarnation of Ajo Gomchen, the aged and revered "great meditator" who presided over Tsognie and my wedding in 1974 and died soon thereafter. In the spring of 2024, Tulku Pema, who was visiting from Sikkim, blessed us during our fiftieth wedding anniversary. Tulku, a celibate monk, is the highly regarded abbot of Enchey Monastery.

Three of Kaden's younger brothers had hugely successful careers in government, serving in myriad capacities, with each rising to secretary level, the highest position in the Sikkim civil service. One of these brothers, Kunga Nima, resigned his post to enter politics on an anti-corruption platform. At times an opposition party of one, he eventually was able to form a successful coalition that in 2019 defeated a well-ensconced incumbent who had served as chief minister for twenty-five years. As an elected senior minister, Kunga held some of the most important portfolios in the newly formed government.

Kaden's younger sister Lhakden served for more than forty years as a teacher and later as headmistress of the Tathanchen School, founded by Zhungkiang in 1961 to serve the children of palace staff and less fortunate children who lived in the vicinity. After her retirement in 2005, she was replaced by one of Tsognie's cousins, Yangchen, who continues to serve as headmistress.

One of two doctors in the family, Tsognie's cousin, Dr. Yangki Shipmo, trained at the prestigious All India Institute and later became the dean of anesthesiologists in Sikkim. For some years, in the mid-eighties, she was the only anesthesiologist in neighboring Bhutan, where she also served as the personal physician to Rani Chuni Dorje, mother to the third king's queen and grandmother to the fourth king. Rani Chuni, who lived to the ripe age of ninety-seven, was the sister of Tashi Namgyal, eleventh ruler of Sikkim.

Members of the younger generation, some unborn at the time the accompanying family photograph was taken, have developed successful careers in medicine, engineering, education, business, the arts, and government service.

No one enters their mid-seventies without having experienced joy, love, sadness, loss, and renewal. Our minds are continually active on many levels—no matter what we are doing. Tsognie and I are never in our garden without thinking about the people, places, and experiences that have shaped our lives. They all reside in our garden, not only in those things that can be seen, but those that dwell in the realm that exists beyond earth and sky.

OPPOSITE
*Tsognie's highly successful maternal Shipputso family, with me at far right, winter 1980–81.*

# PLANT LIST

## JAPANESE MAPLES

*Acer japonicum* 'Aconitifolium' (full moon or fern leaf maple)
*A. japonicum* 'Autumn Moon' (autumn moon maple)
*A. japonicum* 'Green Cascade' (purple maple)
*Acer palmatum* 'Aratama' (dwarf Japanese maple)
*A. palmatum* 'Beni Komachi' (Japanese maple)
*A. palmatum* (bloodgood Japanese maple)
*A. palmatum* 'Beni Shichihenge' (pink and green var. foliage)
*A. palmatum* 'Butterfly' (Butterfly Japanese maple)
*A. palmatum* 'Corallinum' (corallinum pink Japanese maple)
*A. palmatum* 'Emperor 1' (emperor Japanese maple)
*A. palmatum* 'Green Cascade' (weeping full moon maple)
*A. palmatum* 'Little Leaf' (dwarf Japanese maple)
*A. palmatum* 'Crimson Queen' (laceleaf Japanese maple)
*A. palmatum* 'Inaba Shidare' (red weeping laceleaf Japanese maple)
*A. palmatum* 'Jiro Shidare (Japanese maple)
*A. palmatum* 'Hogyoku' (green Japanese maple)
*A. palmatum* 'Kashima' (dwarf Japanese maple)
*A. palmatum* 'Katsura (katsura Japanese maple)
*A. palmatum* 'Kiyohime' (dwarf Japanese maple)
*A. palmatum* 'Koto Hime' (kotohime Japanese maple)
*A. palmatum* 'Kurui Jishi' (crazy lion Japanese maple)
*A. palmatum* 'Lionheart' (laceleaf Japanese maple)
*A. palmatum* 'Nikishi Gawa' (pinebark Japanese maple)
*A. palmatum* 'Mikawa Yatsubusa'(dwarf Japanese maple)
*A. palmatum* 'Murasaki Kiyohime' (dwarf Japanese maple)
*A. palmatum* 'Octopus' (red dwarf weeping Japanese maple)
*A. palmatum* 'Orangeola' (Japanese maple)
*A. palmatum* 'Oshio Beni' (red Japanese maple)
*A. palmatum* 'Red Pigmy (thread leaf Japanese maple)
*A. palmatum* 'Red Select' (weeping Japanese maple)
*A. palmatum* 'Sango Kaku' (coral bark maple)
*A. palmatum* 'Seiryu' (Japanese maple)
*A. palmatum* 'Shaina' (dwarf red Japanese maple)
*A. palmatum* 'Shirasawanum' (golden full moon maple)
*A. palmatum* 'Shishigashira (lion's head Japanese maple)
*A. palmatum* 'Takinogawa' (full moon Japanese maple)
*A. palmatum* 'Tamukeyama' (Japanese maple)
*A. palmatum* 'Tiny Leaf' (tiny leaf Japanese maple)
*A. palmatum* 'Tobiesho' (red Japanese maple)
*A. palmatum* 'Yatsabusa' (dwarf upright Japanese maple)
*A. palmatum* 'Waterfalls' (weeping green laceleaf Japanese maple)
*Acer palmatum* var. *dissectum* 'Green' (green Japanese maple)
*A. palmatum* var. *dissectum* 'Inaba Shidare' (red select cutleaf Japanese maple)
*A. palmatum* var.*dissectum* 'Red' (red Japanese maple)
*A. palmatum* var. *dissectum* 'Red Filigree' (red filigree Japanese maple)
*A. palmatum* var. *dissectum* 'Green' (green Japanese maple)
*A. palmatum* var. *dissectum* 'Koto No Ito' (cutleaf Japanese maple)
*A. palmatum* var. *dissectum* 'Red Dragon' (laceleaf Japanese maple)
*A. palmatum* var. *dissectum* 'Seiryu' (Seiryu Japanese maple)
*A. palmatum* var. *dissectum* 'Viridis' (laceleaf Japanese maple)

## DECIDUOUS TREES

*Acer buergerianum* (trident maple)
*Acer griseum* (paperbark maple)
*Acer pensylvanicum* (moosewood maple)
*Betula nigra* 'Little King' (dwarf river birch)
*B. nigra* 'Heritage' (heritage river birch)
*Betula utilis* var. *jacquemontii* (whitebarked Himalayan birch)
*Boswellia sacra* (incense tree)
*Carpinus betulus* 'Ironwood' (European hornbeam)
*C. betulus* 'Pendula' (weeping European hornbeam)
*Cercidiphyllum japonicum* (katsura tree)
*Cercis canadensis* 'Covey' (Eastern redbud)
*C. canadensis* 'Flamethrower' (Eastern redbud )
*C. canadensis* 'Ruby Falls' (weeping redbud)
*Cercis chinensis* 'Avondale' (Chinese redbud)
*Chionanthus virginius* (fringe tree)
*Chionanthus retusus* (Chinese fringe tree)

*Cornus alternifolia* (pagoda dogwood)
*Cornus kousa* (Chinese dogwood)
*C. kousa* 'Lustgarten' (weeping kousa dowgwood)
*Cornus mas* 'Golden Glory' (cornelian cherry)
*Cornus officinalis* (Japanese cornel)
*Corylus avellana* 'Contorta' (Harry Lauder's walking stick)
*Fagus sylvatica* 'Asplenifolia' (fernleaf beech)
*F. sylvatica* 'Pendula' (weeping beech)
*F. sylvatica* 'Purpurea Pendula' (weeping purple European beech)
*F. sylvatica* 'Rohanii' (purple European beech)
*F. sylvatica* 'Tricolor' (tricolor beech)
*Ginkgo biloba* 'Gold Spire' (gingko tree)
*G. biloba* 'Jade Butterflies' (maidenhair tree)
*G. biloba* 'Merikan' (dwarf globular ginkgo)
*Gleditsia triacanthos* (common honey locust)
*G. triacanthos* var. *inermis* 'Shademaster' (honey locust)
*Halesia carolina* (Carolina silverbell)
*Juglans regia* (Carpathian English walnut)
*Liquidambar styraciflua* 'Slender Silhouette' (slender sweetgum)
*L. styraciflua* 'Worplesdon' (Worplesdon sweetgum)
*Magnolia macrophylla* (big leaf magnolia)
*Magnolia stellata* 'Royal Star' (royal star magnolia)
*Magnolia* x 'Jane' (purple magnolia)
*Quercus xwarei* 'Regal Prince Oak' (columnar oak)
*Quercus alba* (white oak)
*Quercus bicolor* (swamp white oak)
*Querus macrocarpa* (bur oak)
*Quercus phellos* (willow oak)
*Quercus robur* 'Argenteo Marginata' (variegated English oak)
*Quercus rubra* 'Regal Prince' (northern red oak)
*Ponicirus trifoliata* (flying dragon tree)
*Salic acutifolia* (Siberian willow)
*Salix babylonica* 'Scarlet Curls' (scarlet curls willow)
*Salix udensis* 'Sekka' (Japanese fantail willow)
*Stewartia pseudocamellia* (Japanese stewartia)
*Styrax japonica* 'Pendula' (weeping Japanese snowbell)
*Ulmus parvifolia* 'Allee' (lacebark elm)
*Zelkova serrata* 'Ogon' (golden Japanese zelkova)
*Z. serrata* 'Goshiki' (variegated Japanese zelkova)

## DECIDUOUS CONIFERS

*Larix kaempferi* (Japanese larch)
*Metasequoia glyptostroboides* (dawn redwood)
*M. glyptostroboides* 'Amber Glow' (amber glow dawn redwood)
*M. glyptostroboides* 'Gold Rush' (gold rush dawn redwood)
*M. glyptostroboides* 'Sheridan Spire' (Sheridan spire dawn redwood)
*Sequoiadendron giganteum* (giant sequoia)
*S. giganteum* 'Glauca' (blue giant sequoia)
*Taxodium distichum* var. *distichum* (bald cypress)
*Taxodium distichum* 'Green Whisper' (green whisper bald cypress)

## EVERGREEN TREES

*Abies homolepis* (Nikko fir)
*Abies koreana* (Korean fir)
*A. koreana* 'Horstmann's Silberlocke' (Horstmann's Silberlocke spruce)
*Abies lasiodcarpa* ' Glauca Compacta' (blue Arizona cork bark fir)
*Abies nordmanniana* (Caucasian fir)
*A. nordmanniana* 'Tortifolia' (Caucasian fir)
*Abies pinsapo* (Spanish fir)
*Abies procera* (noble fir)
*A. procera* 'Glauca' (blue noble fir)
*Cedrus atlantica* 'Fastigiata' (columnar Atlantic cedar)
*C. atlantica* 'Glauca' (blue atlas cedar)
*Cedrus libani* 'Glauca Pendula' (Lebanon weeping cedar)
*Cedrus deodara* (deodar cedar)
*C. deodara* 'Aurea' (golden deodar cedar)
*C. deodara* 'Kashmir' (Kashmir deodar cedar)
*C. deodara* 'Miles High' (weeping Himalayan cedar)
*C. deodara* 'Prostrate Beauty' (deodar cedar)
*Cephalotaxus harringtonia* 'Fastigiata' (upright plum yew)
*Calocedrus decurrens* (California incense cedar)
*Chamaecyparis lawsoniana* (Lawson cypress)
*C. lawsoniana* 'Golden King' (gold Lawson cypress)
*Chamaecyparis nooktatensis* 'Green Arrow' (narrow weeping Alaskan cedar)
*C. nootkatensis* 'Pendula' (nootka false cypress)
*Chamaecyparis obtusa* 'Aurea Nana' (golden hinoki cypress)
*C. obtusa* 'Crippsii' (golden hinoki false cypress)
*C. obtusa* 'Compacta' (compact hinoki cypress)
*C. obtusa* 'Gracilis' (hinoki cypress)
*C. obtusa* 'Nana Gracilis' (hinoki cypress)
*C. obtusa* 'Kosteri' (Koster's false hinoki cypress)
*C. obtusa* 'Rezek' (slow growing hinoki cypress)
*C. obtusa* 'Rainbow' (rainbow cypress)
*C. obtusa* 'Tempelhof' (hinoki cypress)
*C. obtusa* 'Tetragona Aurea' (golden fernleaf cypress)
*C. obtusa* 'Torulosa' (semi-dwarf cypress)
*C. obtusa* 'Filicoides' (slender hinoki cypress)
*Chamaecyparis pisifera* 'Boulevard' (semi-dwarf boulevard cypress)
*C. pisifera* 'Ericoides' (heath like sawara cypress
*C. pisifera* 'Filifera' (sawara cypress)
*C. pisifera* 'Filifera Aurea' (golden threadleaf sawara cypress)
*C. pisifera* 'Filifera Variegata' (threadleaf false cypress)
*C. pisifera* 'Mini Variegata' (variegated false cypress)
*Cryptomeria japonica* 'Black Dragon' (Japanese cedar)
*C. japonica* 'Gyokuyu' (Japanese cedar)
*C. japonica* 'Radicans' (Japanese cedar)
*C. japonica* 'Yoshino' (Japanese cedar)
*Cupressus arizonica* var. *glabra* 'Blue Ice' (smooth Arizona cypress)
*Cupressus nootkatensis* 'Glaua Pendula' (weeping Alaskan cedar)
*Ilex aquifolium* (English holly)
*Ilex x attenuata* 'Fosteri' (Foster holly)
*Ilex crenata* 'Steeds' (hpright holly)
*Ilex opaca* 'Maryland Dwarf' (dwarf spreader holly)
*I. opaca* 'Greenleaf' (greenleaf American holly)
*I. opaca* 'Miss Helen' (Miss Helen American holly)
*I. opaca* 'Patterson' (Patterson American holly)
*I. opaca* 'Satyr Hill' (satyr hill American holly)
*Ilex meserveae* 'Blue Maid' (blue maid holly)
*Ilex* x 'Dr.Kassab' (Dr. Kassab holly)
*Ilex* x 'Nellie Stevens' (Nellie Stevens holly)
*Ilex* x *aquipernyi* 'Dragon Lady' (dragon lady holly)
*Juniper chinensis* 'Blue Point' (blue point juniper)
*J. chinensis* 'Torulosa' (Hollywood juniper)
*Magnolia grandiflora* 'Alta' (Southern magnolia)
*M. grandiflora* 'Bracken's Brown Beauty' (Southern magnolia)
*M. grandiflora* 'Edith Bogue' (Edith Bogue magnolia)
*M. grandiflora* 'Little Gem' (little gem magnolia)
*Picea abies* (Norway spruce)
*P. abies* 'Cupressina' (fastigiate spruce)
*P. abies* 'Ohlendorfii' (dwarf Norway spruce)
*P. abies* 'Pendula' (weeping Norway spruce)
*Picea jezoensis* subsp. *hondoensis* (Jezo spruce)
*Picea omorika* (Serbian spruce)
*P. omorika* 'Nana' (compact Serbian spruce)
*Picea orientalis* (Oriental spruce)
*P. orientalis* 'Gracilis' (dwarf Oriental spruce)
*P. orientalis* 'Gowdy' (Gowdy Oriental spruce)
*P. orientalis* 'Gracilis Nana' (dwarf Norway spruce)
*P. orientalis* 'Skylands' (golden Oriental spruce)

*Picea pungens* 'Bakeri' (Baker's blue spruce)
*P. pungens* 'Blue Select' (blue select blue spruce)
*P. pungens* 'Glauca Globosa' (dwarf globe blue spruce)
*P. pungens* 'Foxtail' (Colorado spruce)
*P. pungens* 'Hoopsii' (Hoop's blue spruce)
*P. pungens* 'Moerheim' (Moerheim Colorado spruce)
*Picea sitchensis* 'Papoose' (sitka spruce)
*Pinus aristata* (Rocky Mountain bristlecone pine)
*Pinus bungeana* (silver ghost lacebark pine)
*Pinus cembra* (Swiss stone pine)
*Pinus densiflora* 'Globosa' (Japanese red pine)
*P. densiflora* 'Oculus Draconis' (dragon's eye pine)
*P. densiflora* 'Umbraculifera' (umbrella pine)
*Pinus heldreichii* (Bosnian pine)
*Pinus koraiensis* (Korean pine)
*Pinus leucodermis* (Bosnian Pine)
*Pinus mugo* 'Fastigiata' (slow-growing mugo pine)
*Pinus nigra* 'Oregon Green' (Oregon green Austrian pine)
*Pinus parviflora* 'Mount Vernon' (Japanese white pine)
*P. parviflora* 'Nana' (Dwarf Japanese white pine)
*Pinus* pinea (Italian stone pine)
*Pinus resinosa* 'Witches Broom' (witches broom red pine)
*Pinus strobus* 'Blue Shag' (blue shag Eastern white pine)
*P. strobus* 'Contorta' (contorted white pine)
*P. strobus* 'Fastigiata' (Eastern white pine)
*P. strobus* 'Nana' (dwarf white pine)
*P. strobus* 'Pendula' (weeping white pine)
*P. strobus* 'Torulosa' (twisted Eastern white pine)
*Pinus sylvestris* 'Globosa Viridis' (dwarf Scots pine)
*Pinus thunbergii* 'Banshosho' (slow-growing Japanese black pine)
*P. thunbergii* 'Oculus Draconis' (dragon's eye Japanese black pine)
*P. thunbergii* 'Thunderhead' (Japanese black pine)
*Pinus virginiana* 'Wates Gold' (golden Virginia pine)
*Pinus wallichiana* (Bhutan Himalayan pine)
*Pseudotsuga menziesii* 'Pendula' (weeping Douglas fir)
*Sciadopitys verticillata* (Japanese umbrella pine)
*Taxus* x *media* 'Beanpole' (small upright yew)
*Thuja occidentalis* 'De Groots' (DeGroots spire arborvitae)
*T. occidentalis* 'Emerald Green' (emerald giant arborvitae)
*Thuja plicata* 'Green Giant' (giant arborvitae)
*Thuja plicata* 'Steeple Chase' (steeple chase arborvitae)
*Tsuga canadensis* 'Albospica' (white tipped Canadian hemlock)
*T. canadensis* 'Pendula' (Sargent's weeping hemlock)
*T. canadensis* 'Hussi' (Hussi Canadian hemlock)

## EVERGREEN SHRUBS

*Abies pinsapo* 'Nana' (dwarf Spanish rir)
*Buxus microphylla* 'Compacta' (Kingsville dwarf boxwood)
*B. microphylla* 'Grace Henrick Phillips' (littleleaf boxwood)
*Buxus sempervirens* 'Aureovariegata' (variegated boxwood)
*B. sempervirens* 'Vardar Valley' (compact boxwood)
*B. sempervirens* 'Variegata (variegated boxwood)
*B. sempervirens* 'Variegated Globe' (English globe boxwood)
*Buxus sinica* 'Franklin's Gem' (dwarf boxwood)
*Buxus sinica* var. *insularis* 'Nana' (low-spreading boxwood)
*Buxus* x 'Green Mountain' (Green Mountain boxwod)
*Cedrus deodara* 'Prostrate Beauty' (horizontal blue dedar)
*Chamaecyparis obtusa* 'Nana Lutea' (dwarf hinoki)
*C. obtusa* 'Rezek' (Rezek dwarf hinoki)
*C. obtusa* 'Split Rock' (dwarf hinoki cypress)
*C. obtusa* 'Tsatsumi Gold' (golden whorl hinoki)
*Cryptomeria japonica* 'Dragon Warrior' (Japanese cedar)
*C. japonica* 'Dragon Prince' (compact Japanese cedar)
*Ilex compacta* (dense foliage holly)
*Ilex cornuta* 'Burfordii Nana' (dwarf Buford holly)
*Ilex crenata* 'Beehive' (compact Japanese holly)
*I. crenata* 'Chesapeake' (upright Japanese holly)
*I. crenata* 'Drops of Gold' (golden Japanese holly)
*I. crenata* 'Dwarf Pagoda' (pagoda bonsai Japanese holly)
*I. crenata* 'Hoogendorn' (compact Japanese holly)
*I. crenata* 'Soft 'Touch' (dense Japanese holly)
*Ilex glabra* (shamrock inkberry)
*Ilex helleri* (dwarf Japanese holly)
*Ilex* x *meserveae* "Blue Prince' (blue prince holly)
*I.* x *meserveae* 'Blue Princess' (blue princess holly)
*I.* x *meserveae* 'Blue Maid' (blue maid holly)
*I.* x *meserveae* 'China Boy' (China boy holly)
*Juniperus chinensis* 'Plumosa Aurea' (spreading juniper)
*J. chinensis* 'Saybrook Gold' (spreading juniper)
*Juniperus conferta* 'All Gold' (shore juniper)
*J. conferta* 'Blue Pacific' (shore juniper
*Juniperus horizontalis* 'All Gold' (all gold shore juniper)
*Juniperus* x *pfitzeriana* 'Golden Joy' (golden joy juniper)
*Juniperus procumbens* 'Nana' (dwarf Japanese garden juniper)
*Juniperus pulmosa* 'Aurea' (golden plume juniper)
*Juniperus squamata* 'Parsonii' (spreading juniper)
*J. squamata* 'Blue Star' (blue star juniper)
*Ligustrum japonicum* (privet)
*Mahonia aquifolium* (Oregon grape mahonia)
*Osmanthus heterophyllis* 'Kaori Hime' (holly tea olive)
*Picea abies* 'Pygmaea' (dwarf blue spruce shrub)
*Picea bicolor* 'Howell's Dwarf Tigertail' (dwarf Alcock's spruce)
*Picea mariana* 'Nana (dwarf black spruce)
*Picea omorika* 'Nana' (dwarf Serbian spruce)
*Picea pungens* 'Blue Mist' (Colorado spruce)
*P. pungens* 'Compacta' (compact blue spruce)
*P. pungens* 'Glauca Prostrata' (prostrate Colorado blue spruce)
*P. pungens* 'Montgomery (slow-growing dwarf spruce)
*P. pungens* 'Prostrata' (blue spruce)
*Pinus banksiana* 'Uncle Fogy' (weeping jack pine)
*Pinus densiflora* 'Heavy Bud' (heavy bud Japanese red pine)
*Pinus flexilis* 'Glauca' (Rocky Mountain pine)
*P. flexilis Glauca* 'Vanderwolf Pyramid' (pyramid limber pine)
*Pinus mugo* 'Golden Glow' (golden mugo pine)
*P. mugo* 'Hesse' (Hesse dwarf mountain pine)
*P. mugo* 'Mops' (dwarf mountain pine)
*P. mugo* 'Nippon Glow' (golden glow mugo pine)
*P. mugo* 'Palouse' (TRUdwarf palouse mugo pine)
*P. mugo* 'Prostrata Wells' (Swiss mountain pine)
*P. mugo* ' Slow Mound' (compact mugo pine)
*P. mugo* var. 'Pumilio (Dwarf Swiss mountain pine)
*Pinus nigra* 'Hornibrookiana' (dwarf Austrian pine)
*P. nigra* 'Oregon Green' (Oregon green Austrian pine)
*Pinus parviflora* 'Adcock's Dwarf' (slow-growing Japanese white pine)
*Pinus pumila* (Siberian dwarf pine)
*Pinus pungens* 'Hoopsi 16' (Colorado spruce)
*Pinus resinosa* 'Witches Broom' (red pine)
*Pinus strobus* 'Hershey' (dwarf Eastern white pine)
*P. strobus* 'Nana' (dwarf Eastern white pine)
*Pinus sylvestris* 'Dwarf Scotch Pine' (dwarf Scotch pine)
*P. sylvestris* 'Beuvronensis' (dwarf globe Scotch pine)
*P. sylvestris* 'Glauca Nana' (dwarf Scotch pine)
*P. sylvestris* 'Hillside Creeper' (Scotch pine)
*P. sylvestris* 'Moseri' (dwarf yellow Scotch pine)
*Pinus thunbergii* 'Ogon' (Japanese Black pine)
*P. thunbergii* 'Thunderhead' (thunderhead pine)
*P. thunbergii* 'Yatsubusa' (dwarf Japanese black pine)
*Pseudotsuga menziesii* (dwarf Douglas fir)
*Taxus baccata* 'Fowle's Dwarf' (dwarf compact yew)
*Thuja occidentalis* 'Hoseri' (American arbovitae)

## FLOWERING SHRUBS

*Abelia* x *grandiflora* 'Kaleidoscope' (glossy abelia)
*A.* x *grandiflora* 'Radiance' (radiance abelia)
*Buddleia* 'Grand Cascade' (lavender butterfly bush)
*B.* x 'Black Knight' (dark violet butterfly bush)
*B.* x 'Glass Slippers' (summer lilac butterfly bush)
*B.* x 'Miss Molly' (sangria red butterfly bush)
*B.* x 'Pugster Amethyst' (light purple butterfly bush)
*B.* x 'Pugster Blue' (blue butterfly bush)
*B.* x 'Pugster White' (dwarf butterfly bush)
*B.* x 'Cranrazz' (cran-raspberry butterfly bush)
*B.* 'Grand Cascade' (light lavender butterfly bush)
*Calluna vulgaris* (multicolor common heather)
*Corylopsis glabrescens* (fragrant winter hazel)
*Daphne* x *burkwoodii* 'Carol Mackie' (fragrant daphne)
*D. x burkwoodii* 'Bricks Moonlight' (cream-colored daphne)
*Daphne cneorum* (rose daphne)
*Daphne odora* (winter daphne)
*Hamamelis mollis* 'Pallida' (yellow witch hazel)
*H.* x *intermedia* 'Primavera' (bright yellow witch hazel)
*Hibiscus syriacus* 'Purpureus Varegatus' (variegated rose of sharon)
*Hydrangea aspera* (lavender white hydragea)
*Hydrangea macrophilla* 'Tokyo Delight' (big-leaf hydrangea)
*Hydrangea petiolaris* (climbing hydrangea)
*Hydrangea* 'Schizophraga' (Japanese hydrangea vine)
*Ilex* x 'Sparkleberry' (winterberry)
*Ilex verticillata* 'Apollo' (holly pollinator)
*I. verticillata* 'Winter Gold' (winterberry)
*Kalmia latifolia (*dwarf mountain laurel*)*
*Kerria japonica (*double-flowering Japanese kerria)
*Paeonia ostii* 'Feng DanBai'(Phoenix White tree peony)
*Paeonia* x *suffruticosa* 'Lan Bao Shi' (Chinese tree peony)
*P.* x *suffruticosa* 'Kao' (Japanese tree peony)
*P.* x *suffruticosa* (red tree peony)
*P.* x *suffruticosa* (purple tree peony)
*P.* x *suffruticosa* (white tree peony)
*Pieris japonica* 'Mountain Fire' (mountain fire andromeda)
*P. japonica* 'Prelude' (pink andromeda)
*Spirea bumalda* 'Gold Mound' (goldmound spirea)
*Spirea* 'Double Play' (candy corn spirea)
*Spirea* 'Magic Carpet'
*Viburnum* x *burkwoodii* (Burkood viburnum)
*Viburnum* x *carlecephalum* 'Cayuga' (Koreanspice viburnum)
*Wisteria floribunda* 'Alba' (white wisteria)
*W. floribunda* (blue/purple wisteria)

## ROSES

*Rosa banksiae* 'Alba Plena' (white Lady Banks climbing rose)
*Rosa* 'Candy Land' (pink and white climbing rose)
*R.* 'Double Knock Out' (red rose)
*R.* 'Meidevi' (Buttercream Drift groundcover rose)
*R.* 'Meiggili' (Peach Drift groundcover rose)
*R.* 'Meijocos' (Pink Drift groundcover rose)
*R.* 'Meiswetdom' (Sweet Drift pink groundcover rose)
*R.* 'New Dawn' (pink climbing rose)
*R.* 'Novarospop' (Popcorn Drift yellow/white groundcover rose)
*R.* 'Peach Star' (Peach Star Drift Rose)
*R. rugosa* (seaside rose)
*R.* 'Salley Holmes' (ivory-white shrub rose)
*R.* 'William Baffin' #5 (climbing pink rose)
*R.* 'Winner's Circle' (climbing red rose)
*R.* 'Zephirine Drouhin' (deep pink climbing rose)

## RHODODENDRONS & AZALEAS

*Azalea* 'Aphrodite'
*A. arborescens* (sweet azalea)
*A.* 'Autumn Sundance'
*A.* 'Cannon's Double' (double azalea)
*A.* 'Caroline Gable'
*A.* 'Elsie Lee'
*A.* 'Encore Sunset'
*A.* 'Exbury'
*A.* 'Flame'
*A.* 'Girard's Hot Shot'
*A.* 'Girard's Purple'
*A.* 'Girard's Renee Michelle'
*A.* 'Gumpo White'
*A.* 'Gumpo Pink'
*A.* 'Hino Crimson' (Kurume Hybrid)
*A.* 'Lord Roberts'
*A.* 'Mootum Autumn Light'
*A.* 'Red'
*A.* 'Rose Bud'
*A.* 'Sir Robert' (dwarf azalea)
*A.* 'Silver Sword'
*A.* 'White Incan'
*Rhododendron* 'Calsap'
*Rhododendron catawbiense* 'Album Elegans'
*R. catawbiense* 'Grandiflorum' (catawba rhododendrom)
*R. catawbiense* 'Roseum Elegans'
*R.* 'Conlee Autumn Amethyst' (evergreen azalea)
*R.* 'Conlee Autumn Sunset'
*R.* 'Conlee Autumn Royalty'
*R. maximum* (native rhododendron)
*R. roblec* 'Autumn Carnation'
*R.* 'Cunningham
*R.* x 'English Roseum'
*R.* 'Nova Zembla'
*R.* 'Roseum Elegans'
*R.* 'Percy Wiseman'

## FRUIT TREES

*Malus* 'Salish' (apple)
M. 'Vigoro' (espalier apple)
M. 'Sargenti' (Sargent crabapple)
*Prunus persica* 'Avalon Pride' (sweet peach)
*P. persica* 'Bounty' (bounty peach)
*P. persica* 'Desiree' (peach)
*P. persica* 'Rich May' (Rich May peach)
*P. persica* 'Salish Summer' (Salish summer peach)
*Prunus salicina* (Japanese Rosa Plum Dwarf)
*P. salicina* (Japanese plum)
*Pyrus pyrifolia* (Hosui Asian pear)
*P. pyrifolia* (dwarf Raja Asian pear)

## PERENNIALS

*Calluna vulgaris* (Heather Erica)
*Helleborus x hybridus* 'Double Vision' (Lenten rose)
*H. x hybridus* 'First Dance' (palmlike Lenten rose)
*H. x hybridus* 'Red Lady'
*H.* x *hybridus* 'Sun Flair'
*Hemerocallis* 'Hyperion' (yellow daylily)
*H.* 'Ming To' (orange-red daylily)
*Iris ensata* 'Anytus' (white Japanese iris)
*I. ensata* 'Bellender (blue water Japanese iris)
*I. ensata* 'Crystal Halo' (maroon and white-edged Japanese iris)

*I. ensata* ‘Frosted Intrigue’ (deep purple and white Japanese iris)
*I. ensata* ‘Jocasta’ (blended dark purple Japanese iris)
*I. ensata* ‘Lion King’ (red and white Japanese iris)
*I. ensata* ‘Moonlight Waves’ (Japanese iris)
*I. ensata* ‘Ruffled Whitewater’ (Japanese iris)
*I. ensata* ‘Second Wave’ (Japanese iris)
*I. ensata* ‘Tea Ceremony’ (red and white iris Japanese iris)
*Iris germanica* ‘Bernice Legacy’ (bearded iris)
*I. germanica* ‘Champagne Elegans’ (bearded iris)
*I. germanica* ‘Enthralled Bearded’ (bearded iris)
*I. germanica* ‘Going Green’ (bearded iris)
*I. germanica* ‘Immortality’ (bearded iris)
*I. germanica* ‘Kissed by the Sun’ (bearded iris)
*I. germanica* ‘Lovely Senorita’ (bearded iris)
*I. germanica* ‘Montmartre’ (bearded iris)
*I. germanica* ‘Ultimate’ (bearded iris)
*I. germanica* ‘Outspoken’ (bearded iris)
*I. germanica* ‘Paprika Fonos’ (bearded iris)
*I. germanica* ‘Pride of Ireland’ (bearded iris)
*I. germanica* ‘Pure as Gold’ (bearded iris)
*I. germanica* ‘Protocol’ (bearded iris)
*I. germanica* ‘Sorbonne Reblooming’ (bearded iris)
*I. germanica* ‘War Chief’ (bearded iris)
*I. germanica* ‘Wild Angel’ (bearded iris)
*I. germanica* ‘Ziggy Reblooming’ (bearded iris)
*Iris pseudata* ‘Akimatsuri’ (yellow water Iris)
*Iris sibirica* ‘Activity’ (Siberian iris)
*I. sibirica* ‘Black Joker’ (Siberian iris)
*I. sibirica* ‘Butter and Sugar’ (Siberian iris)
*I. sibirica* ‘Caesar’s Brother’ (Siberian iris)
*I. sibirica* ‘Conord Crush’ (Siberian iris)
*I. sibirica* ‘Crystal Halo’ (Siberian iris)
*I. sibirica* ‘Flying Fiddles’ (Siberian iris)
*I. sibirica* ‘Miss Apple’ (Siberian iris)
*I. sibirica* ‘Royal Banner’ (Siberian iris)
*I. sibirica* ‘So Van Gogh’ (Siberian iris)
*I. sibirica* ‘Swans in Flight’ (Siberian iris)
*Lilium* ‘Lionheart’ (Asiatic lily)
*Lupinus polyphyllus* ‘Masterpiece’ (Westcountry ‘Masterpiece’ lupine)
*Lysimachia japonica* ‘Minutissima’ (miniature moneywort)
*Mentha spicata* ‘Kentucky Colonel’ (mint)
*Pachysandra procumbens*
*Sarcococca confusa* (sweet box)
*Sarracenia* ‘Creeper Island’ (pitcher plant)
*Selaginella kraussiana* (green spikemoss)
*S. kraussiana* ‘Aurea’ (gold spikemoss)
*Vinca minor* “Ralph Shugert’ (lesser periwinkle)

## ORNAMENAL GRASSES & BAMBOO

*Fargesia* (clump bamboo)
*Hakonechloa macra* ‘Aureola’ (golden hakonechloa)

## FERNS

*Adiantum pedatum* (maidenhair fern)
*Cyrtomium falcatum* ‘Rochfordianum’ (Japanese holly fern)
*Cyrtomium fortunei* (fortune’s holly fern)
*Dryopteris erythrosora* (autumn fern)
*Polystichum acrostichoides* (Christmas fern)
*Polystichum tsus-simense* (Korean rock fern)

## TROPICALS

*Ixora* species
*Nephrolepsis obliterata* (queen fern)

# SUGGESTED READING

## INSPIRATION


Anderson, Nola. *Immersion: Living and Learning in an Olmsted Garden*. Damiani Books, 2021.

Clarke, Victoria, editor. *Garden: Exploring the Horticultural World*. Phaidon Press, 2023.

Cook, Diane, and Len Jenshel. *Wise Trees*. Abrams, 2017.

Darke, Rick. *The American Woodland Garden: Capturing the Spirt of the Deciduous Forest*. Timber Press, 2002.

Durham, Mignon. *Devotion: Diary of an Appalachian Garden*. Mignon Durham Industries, 2021.

Ewing, William. *Flora Photographica: Masterpieces of Flower Photography*. Thames & Hudson, 1991.

Fryberger, Betsy G. *The Changing Garden: Four Centuries of European and American Art*. University of California Press, 2003.

Hudson, Kathy. *On Walnut Hill: The Evolution of a Garden*. Hillside Press, 2015.

Impelluso, Lucia. *Gardens in Art*. J. Paul Getty Museum, 2007.

Lederman, Larry. *Magnificent Trees of the New York Botanical Garden*. Monacelli Press and New York Botanical Garden, 2012.

Lederman, Larry, Cynthia B. Altman, and Todd Forrest. *The Rockefeller Family Gardens: An American Legacy*. Monacelli Press/Phaidon Books, 2017.

Lederman, Larry, and Thomas Christopher. *Garden Portraits: Experiences of Natural Beauty*. Monacelli Press/Phaidon Books, 2020.

Long, Gregory, and Anne Skillion, eds. *The New York Botanical Gardens*. Abrams, 2006.

Marley, Anna O., ed. *The Artist's Garden: American Impressionism and the Garden Movement*. University of Pennsylvania Press, 2015.

McDowell, Marta. *Dupont Gardens of the Brandywine Valley*. Monacelli Press/Phaidon Books, 2023.

McNear, Sarah Anne, and Jamie M. Allen. *The Photographer in the Garden*. Aperture, 2018.

Mullet, Carolyn. *Adventures in Eden: An Intimate Tour of the Private Gardens of Europe*. Timber Press, 2020.

Newhall, Charles W. *Brightside Gardens: A Dialogue Between the Head and the Heart, The Gardens of Amy & Charles W. Newhall, III*. Bibliotheca Brightside, 2017.

Phaidon editors. *The Garden Book*. Phaidon Press, 2022.

Phaidon editors. *Plant: Exploring the Botanical World*. Phaidon Press, 2016.

Seebohm, Caroline. *Sleepy Cat Farm: A Gardener's Journey*. Monacelli Press/Phaidon Books, 2021.

Shigemori, Kanto. *The Japanese Courtyard Garden: Landscapes for Small Spaces*. Weatherhill, 1981.

Staub, Jack. *Private Edens: Beautiful Country Gardens*. Gibbs Smith, 2012.

Stein, Alan, and Nancy Virts. *The Conservatory: Gardens Under Glass*. Princeton Architectural Press, 2021.

*Sukiya Living: The Journal of Japanese Gardening*. http://www.rothteien.com/index.htm.

Watters, Sam, ed. *American Gardens, 1890–1930: Northeast, Mid-Atlantic, and Midwest Region*. Acanthus Press, 2006.

Way, Thaïsa, ed. *Garden As Art: Beatrix Farrand at Dumbarton Oaks*. Dumbarton Oaks Research Library and Collection, 2022.

## AESTHETICS

Cha-Tsu Siu, Victoria M. *Gardens of a Chinese Emperor: Imperial Creations of the Qianlong Era, 1736–1796*. Lehigh University Press, 2013.

Dun-Zhen, Liu. *Chinese Classical Gardens of Suzhou*. China Architecture and Building Press, McGraw-Hill, 1993.

Highland, Chris. *Meditations of John Muir: Nature's Temple*. Wilderness Press, 2010.

Kean, Marc P. *Japanese Garden Notes: A Visual Guide to Elements and Design*. Stone Bridge Press, 2017.

Keswick, Maggie. *The Chinese Garden: History, Art & Architecture*, 2nd revised ed. Frances Lincoln, 2003.

Koren, Leonard. *Wabi-Sabi for Artists, Designers, Poets & Philosophers*. Imperfect Publishing, 2008.

Laurent, Anna. *Botanical Art from the Golden Age of Scientific Discovery*. University of Chicago Press, 2016.

Muir, John. *Spiritual Writings*. Orbis Books, 2013.

Richie, Donald. *A Tractate on Japanese Aesthetics*. Stone Bridge Press, 2007.

Rustomji, Nari. *Enchanted Frontiers: Sikkim, Bhutan, and India's North-Eastern Borderlands*. Oxford University Press, 1972.

Walker, Sophie. *The Japanese Garden*. Phaidon Press, 2017.

## REFERENCE

Beer, Robert. *The Encyclopedia of Tibetan Symbols and Motifs*. Shambhala Press, 1999.

Behler, John. *National Audubon Society Field Guide to North American Reptiles and Amphibians*. Alfred A. Knopf, 1979.

Bitner, Richard L. *Conifers for Gardens: An Illustrated Encyclopedia*. Timber Press, 2007.

Bull, John, and John Farrand. *National Audubon Society Field Guide to North American Birds, Eastern Region*. Alfred A. Knopf, 1994.

Burrell, C. Colston, and Judith Knott Tyler. *Hellebores: A Comprehensive Guide*. Timber Press, 2006.

Dirr, Michael. *Manual of Woody Landscape Plants: Their Identification, Ornamental Characteristics, Propagation, and Uses*. Stipes, 2009.

Flint, Harrison L. *Landscape Plants for Eastern North America*. Wiley, 1997.

Gracie, Carol. *Summer Wildflowers of the Northeast: A Natural History*. Princeton University Press, 2020.

Kuitert, Wybe. *Japanese Flowering Cherries*. Timber Press, 1999.

Lianying, Wang. *Chinese Tree Peony*. The Peony Association of China, China Forestry Publishing House, 1998.

Lincoff, Gary. *National Audubon Society Field Guide to North American Mushrooms*. Alfred A. Knopf, 1981.

Little, Elbert L. *National Audubon Society Field Guide to North American Trees: Eastern Region*. Alfred A. Knopf, 1980.

Meredith, Ted Jordan. *Bamboo for Gardens*. Timber Press, 2006.

Michaux, Francois-André, and Pierre-Joseph Redouté. *The Trees of North America*. With an afterword and additional illustrations by David Allen Sibley. New York Botanical Garden with Abbeville Press, 2017.

Milne, Margery, and Lorus Johnson Milne. *National Audubon Society Field Guide to North American Insects and Spiders*. Alfred A. Knopf, 1980.

Niering, William A. *National Audubon Society Field Guide to North American Wildflowers, Eastern Region*. Alfred A. Knopf, 2001.

Peattie, Donald C. *A Natural History of Trees of Eastern and Central North America*. Houghton Mifflin, 1991.

Poor, Janet Meakin, and Nancy Peterson Brewster, eds. *Plants That Merit Attention, Volume I: Trees*. Timber Press and the Garden Club of America, 1994.

Poor, Janet Meakin, and Nancy Peterson Brewster, eds. *Plants That Merit Attention, Volume II: Shrubs*. Timber Press and the Garden Club of America, 1994.

Sternberg, Guy. *Native Trees for North American Landscapes*. Timber Press, 2004.

Strong, Roy. *A Celebration of Gardens*. Timber Press, 1993.

Tripp, Kim E., and J. C. Raulston. *The Year in Trees: Superb Woody Plants for Four-Season Gardens*. Timber Press, 1995.

Van Gelderen, D. M. *Conifers: The Illustrated Encyclopedia, Volume I, A–K*. Timber Press, 1996.

Van Gelderen, D. M. *Maples of the World*. Timber Press, 1994.

Vertrees J. D. *Japanese Maples: Momiji and Keade*. 3rd ed. Timber Press, 2001.

# ACKNOWLEDGMENTS

THIS BOOK WOULD NOT EXIST were if not for the skill, encouragement, and generosity of photographer and friend Norman Barker. Tsognie and I developed the gardens at Tashiding for the enjoyment of our family and our close friends. There came a point, however, when word of our endeavors got out and we found ourselves hosting numerous garden tours. Seeing our garden through visitors' eyes gave us a somewhat new and different perspective on what we had accomplished. But it wasn't until Norm discovered our garden that the idea of a book began to take form.

In December 2021, Norm and his wife, Barb, joined us for a celebration of life to honor our late mutual friends, Giraud and Carolyn Foster. Norm had never visited Tashiding before but immediately decided that photographing the gardens would make an interesting project. In short order, Norm began a project that, over the past several years, has included well over a hundred working visits and thousands of stunning photographs. His work challenged me to think more deeply about why the gardens developed the way they did. Thus began a collaboration that resulted in *Tashiding: Beyond Earth and Sky*. I will be forever grateful for Norm's friendship and unending energy.

We sent an early version of the proposed book to Elizabeth White of Monacelli Press, an imprint of Phaidon, and she kindly referred us to book producer Jan Hartman of Jan Hartman Books. We retained Jan, who immediately began the process of disassembling much of the material we presented to her then reorganizing and reshaping it to form the coherent and interesting book that exists today. I particularly owe Jan a debt of gratitude for her expertise and professionalism, her toughness when required, and her unwavering dedication to creating a book that I believe will be of interest to many readers.

Jan recruited two talented individuals to our team. Editor Susan Lauzau worked closely with me to polish and improve my writing while maintaining my unique voice throughout the manuscript. I particularly enjoyed our many Friday morning editing sessions that always seemed to end too soon.

The elegant design of *Tashiding: Beyond Earth and Sky* is the work of award-winning graphic designer Sarah Gifford. Incorporating the diverse content of our book into a cohesive and attractive whole was no small task. The finished product is testament to her exceptional talent.

Maryland photographer and friend Paula Reynolds graciously allowed us to include two of her wonderful images in the book. The numerous photographs of Sikkim are from our family collection. Many were digitized from existing photos by Norm Barker. Credit is owed to John Eichelberger for restoring several of the historical photographs. The excellent scale plan of the property on page 22 was prepared and contributed by landscape architect Barbara Hopkins, working with Baltimore County GIS and drone footage generously contributed by photographers Jon Christofersen and James T. VanRensselaer.

Horticulturalist Monika Burwell took on the enormous task of developing a live plant list by organizing our boxes of receipts into a coherent and impressive plant list that will be of interest to many readers.

Publisher Gordon Goff, founder of ORO Editions, recognized the book's value and beauty, and was immediately excited to publish *Tashiding*, marketing and distributing the work through ORO's international network. Jake Anderson, ORO COO, was invaluable in securing superb production values for the book. At Smith Publicity, Kelli Rendina collaborated with the authors and ORO to execute a dynamic publicity and marketing program.

# INDEX

Page numbers for photographs indicate the page of the image; caption may be on an adjacent page.

RIGHT
*My long-term partners in creating and maintaining Tashiding, Efrain Martinez Sosa (left) and Stanley "Hank" Beall (right)*

## PHOTOGRAPHY CREDITS

Principal photography by Norman Barker

Additional photographs by:

Douglas Hamilton: Pages 34, 36, 37 (bottom), 59, 62–63, 64 (top and bottom left), 65, 68–69, 73, 77, 78, 96–97, 134–135, 152, 272, 274, 284–285, 309, 312, 315, 316–317, 322, 324, 326, 329, and 346

Hamilton family photo archive: Pages 37 (bottom), 42, 44–45, 47, 48, 50–51, 52, 58, 60–61, 76, 281 (top and bottom right), 313, and 319

Tom Bradley: Page 35

Margaret Hamilton: Page 41

Tsognie Hamilton: Page 64 (bottom left)

Jon Christofersen: Pages 124 and 270

Paula Reynolds: Pages 141 and 168

Vasant Nayak: Page 276

John Sokolowski: Page 278 (top)

Richard Anderson: Page 279

Palden Hamilton: Oil paintings on pages 173 and 239

ORO Editions
Publishers of Architecture, Art, and Design
Gordon Goff, Publisher

www.oroeditions.com
info@oroeditions.com

Published by ORO Editions


Foreword: Kate Markert
Contributors: Norman Barker, Tsognie Hamilton
Author: Douglas Hamilton Jr.
Book Producer: Jan Hartman, Jan Hartman Books
Editor: Susan Lauzau
Designer: Sarah Gifford
Project Manager: Jake Anderson

COLOPHON
This book is typeset in Maiola, a contemporary font designed by Veronika Burian, distinctive for its historical old-style references and calligraphic expression.

10 9 8 7 6 5 4 3 2 1 First Edition
ISBN: 978-1-961856-86-8

Prepress and Print work by ORO Editions Inc.
Printed in China

ORO Editions makes a continuous effort to minimize the overall carbon footprint of its publications. As part of this goal, ORO, in association with Global ReLeaf, arranges to plant trees to replace those used in the manufacturing of the paper produced for its books. Global ReLeaf is an international campaign run by American Forests, one of the world's oldest nonprofit conservation organizations. Global ReLeaf is American Forests' education and action program that helps individuals, organizations, agencies, and corporations improve the local and global environment by planting and caring for trees.